PURCHASING AND MATERIALS MANAGEMENT

PURCHASING AND MATERIALS MANAGEMENT

DPH Management Series

PURCHASING AND MATERIALS MANAGEMENT

J M DEWAN • K N SUDARSHAN

DISCOVERY PUBLISHING HOUSE
NEW DELHI-110002

Reprinted - 2018

First Published - 1996

ISBN: 978-81-7141-354-6

Purchasing and Materials Management

Published by:

DISCOVERY PUBLISHING HOUSE PVT. LTD.

4383/4B, Ansari Road, Darya Ganj

New Delhi-110 002 (India)

Phone: +91-11-23279245, 43596064-65

Fax: +91-11-23253475

E-mail: discoverypublishinghouse@gmail.com

sales@discoverypublishinggroup.com

web: www.discoverypublishinggroup.com

Printed at:

Infinity Imaging Systems

Delhi

Preface

The management world is in transition. The causes of this transition are many, but the major one is the vast changes in knowledge and in the information that flows in and out of organizations. This changing information disrupts traditions, established processes, well-known procedures, and routine ways of doing things. New principles, concepts, techniques, ideas, expressions, processes, and procedures are emerging, moving us to a new plateau of professional practice. Trying to capture this changing knowledge and information is like trying to capture the atmosphere. How can you do it when the atmosphere is continually shifting and when you need the atmosphere to do the capturing? The best we can do is find a peak from which we can at least get a perspective on management as a whole, decide on the work and responsibilities of management, and gather in whatever practical management information we can. A team of experts in this series represent some of the best contemporary thinking and information available. They represent many major successful corporations, active consulting agencies, and well-known educational institutions, and all are experts on what is happening with the flow of knowledge and information in the management world. This is a lofty pinnacle from which to survey the management world.

Managers and supervisors clamor for current information and guidelines to help solve formidable problems in their work world—problems that range from "how to do it" to "how to resolve conflict when doing it." Many problems are generated from miscommunication and incompetence. As the management practice proceeds from the complex to the supercomplex, problem solving becomes a large-scale challenge requiring new knowledge and skills. Managers and supervisors cannot wait for research breakthroughs with real-world answers to solve these dilemmas. They must tackle them here and now with the useful information and proven practices immediately available. Whether making a decision, solving a problem setting up a procedure, designing a process, or resolving a behaviour conflict, a manager must rely heavily on information. To a great extent, management practitioners are information workers; that is, they generate, distribute, store, retrieve, and consume information. Competence in finding and using the right information at the needed time determines to a considerable extent competence in the management function, activity, or responsibility. The *DPH Management Series* attempts to fill this need for usable information in spite of the changing nature of its subject.

The *DPH Management Series* not a book to be read and later discarded. It is a reference book, a tool to be used by managerial personnel in the day-to-day work of an organization. Like a tool, it should never be more than a reach away when a new situation emerges that demands its use. This series aim to achieve a first-and practical and proven knowledge and information as a self-development opportunity for those who are moving into or upward in management. A complete spectrum of management subjects is immediately available for orientation, study, analysis, assimilation, and problem solving. Within one set of covers is the view of management as a totality. The management field is loaded with ideas that the organization of this handbook series unique logic. It follows both levels and areas of responsibilities of an organization.

The work of this handbook series is the collaborative effort of many outstanding people in the management field. The motivation for this work varied from individual to individual, but the central motivation that united us all was the excitement of capturing the management state-of-the-art and sharing it with colleagues in the dynamic profession of management.

This series should be of great help to managerial practitioners at any organizational level who are responsible for a function, department, or set of responsibilities. The handbook series will also give these practitioners insights into management roles and approaches in other areas as well. The subject matter encompasses top, middle, and lower management. Special emphasis was placed on managing people, time, space, budgets, and resources to give the handbook extra utility for middle and lower management. Students of management in university or educational institutions will find the series an invaluable resource for adding "real world" practices to their academic and theoretical foundations. MBA students will gain an invaluable overview of the total organization to complement their MBA degree. Administrators and public managers can become acquainted with practices employed by managers and supervisors in private organizations. These practices are not always directly applicable in public sector bodies, but with thought and modifications, these private practices can adapt to public organizations. Public and university librarians will find the handbook an indispensable reference for the multitude of questions on many topics from the general public, special groups, associations, and students.

Editors

Contents

1 Purchasing Input/Output Management

Production managers strive to attain organisational goals in various ways. Input control is one of these. Inputs are relatively simple to control; often they deal with repetitive decision problems. A single decision that deviates from the optimal cannot do much harm. Only the cumulative effects of repeated diver-gencies from optimal results can impose severe penalties over a period of time. Therefore, control can be used to keep the system on course.

Process inputs produce direct costs. When lumped together these costs constitute a major share of operating costs. Thus, the inputs are associated with the variable-cost line of the break-even chart. This is the area of cost control that is most familiar to production managers. We shall consider two fundamental kinds of inputs, in this chapter.

The materials system

Many companies have been moving toward an organisational integration of materials control functions. In many firms these activities existed as individual operations each attended by individuals who seldom communicated with each other. Eventually, in the search for greater control, a single, central material control department appeared in numerous organisations.

Today, many organizations will be found to have a vice president in charge of materials control. The responsibilities vested in a materials control department include at least three subfunctions, namely, procurement or purchasing, inventory control, and acceptance sampling. We shall treat each of these topics, and, in addition, we shall briefly discuss the subject of value analysis which is intimately involved with the optimal selection and specification of materials.

It is a flow diagram which depicts the various communications that unite the materials control area. We observe that many forms of communication must flow between the organizational units in order to achieve an integrated materials control departments. In addition, the materials control department communicates with the production division, with other operating divisions of the company, and in many ways with the external world.

Purchasing or procurement

The purchasing division occupies a vital and unique position. Through the procurement function the organization operates as a customer. Accordingly, it is susceptible to the marketing strategies of the vendors from whom it obtains the materials that are required for its operations.

Depending upon the extent to which the company requires outside suppliers and is not self-sufficient- the importance of the buying function increases. For example, a mail order company produces a very small fraction of the materials which it offers for sale. Buyers in such enterprises are responsible, in large measure, for the success of their companies. Commensurate with this responsibility is the remuneration which such buyers receive. At the same time, they must accept the risk of making errors in carrying out their function. The penalties of errors can be high.

It will be impossible to discuss all the intricate relationships that have been developed by buyers and vendors in order to achieve maximum satisfaction for both parties. One important procedure, however, should be mentioned. It is called *vendor releasing*. In this case, a buyer contracts for a substantial number of units and, thereby, obtains discount prices. The vendor agrees to ship specific quantities of the purchased material at stated intervals. By previous arrangement the approximate shipping quantities for each time period are agreed upon. Generally, the buyer is in a position to change the quantities, from time to time, as vendor releasing, is dependent upon a reasonable forecast of demand and a reasonably accurate specification of the vendor's lead time. It requires a fairly long-term commitment to obtain the benefits of quantity discounts.

Vendor relations depend to a great extent on the nature of a company's operations. Bypassing mail order, wholesale and retail inventories, we can divide purchased inventory into two major groups: (1) materials required for production and (2) materials required for maintenance of plant and equipment. With respect to the first class, some companies purchase manufactured and assembled item; other companies deal primarily with basic raw materials and commodity markets. There is a real difference in the purchasing agent's approach to each of these situations.

Let us consider, for example, the green coffee commodity market from the point of view of a coffee producer. A larger than normal inventory may have to be built up at a particular time, as a result of favourable coffee prices. The cost of holding this inventory must be balanced against the advantage to be gained by overbuying. If the problem is one of underbuying while waiting for a more favourable market, then the cost of running out of stock must be taken into account. Under certain circumstances specialized buying techniques may be involved. These include hedging and speculative purchases, both of which require forward buying.

Hedging involves the buying and selling of commodity futures. Thus, a company fearing that commodity prices will rise, buys a given amount of the material for delivery in a future month. The market price is paid plus carrying charges. When the material is actually required for production-before the future month—a spot purchase is made for cash and immediate delivery. Simultaneously a sale is made for delivery in the future month. If the price of the commodity has risen, then the selling price of the future contract reflect this as compared to the buying price of the futures. This point, when applied to the purchase price of the spot transaction, smooths out the rise in price that has occurred. Thus:

1. Our company counts on a raw material cost of $1.00 per pound.
2. Fearing a price rise in this raw material, but having sufficient supply on hand, the purchasing agent buys 1000 pounds for delivery to his company at some specific future date- at $1.03 per pound.
3. After a period of time, prices have risen. The cost per pound is now $1.50. The company requires and buys 100 pounds at this price, expecting rapid delivery.
4. But on the same date, the company agrees to sell 1000 pounds for delivery at the same future date.
5. In this way, the company sells the commodity for future delivery and receives income, on a per pound basis, of $1.53. It has previously purchased material to cover this sale at $1.03. This yields a profit per pound of $0.50.
6. But the company had to pay $1.50 instead of $1.00 per pound to take care of its production requirements-or an increase per pound of $0.50.
7. This results in a net change for our company in the price per pound of $0.0. If the price had

fallen, similar reasoning applies. The company doesn't benefit from the drop in price, but ends up with zero net change.

The purchase of coffee is only one example of this type of situation. We could, as well, have cited the grain commodity market which affects distilleries and flour mills or the cattle commodity market for both meat and skins. Soft-drink manufacturers must adapt their activities to the sugar market. Textile manufacturers deal with cotton commodities. The confectionery industry buys cocoa. Other commodities include rubber, potatoes, zinc, and cottonseed oil.

Commodity buying

Although it is exceedingly complicated, commodity buying can be analyzed in terms of a formal model. We shall present a simple example of such a model with the intention of indicating the conceptual basis upon which the problems can be approached and to highlight the kind of information that is required.

The objective is to minimize the cost of a primary raw material input that is characteristically subject to fluctuating prices.

Step 1. We obtained probability estimates that describe the relative likelihood for different commodity prices in each quarter of the year. Such estimates could be obtained by consulting historical records of the particular commodity market. For simplicity, we class the price by whole dollars and use time breaks of three months. In practice these classes can be made as fine as appears to be warranted.

COST	*Quarters* 1	2	3	4
$4.00	.40	.30	.40	.10
5.00	.40	.30	.30	.40
6.00	.20	.40	.30	.50
Expected cost	$4.80	$5.10	$4.90	$5.40

Step 2. Assume that we have to make one purchase in the year. If we defer buying until the fourth quarter, the expected cost will be $5.40. Can we do better than this? We note that if we buy in the third quarter there is a 70 per cent chance of doing better, viz., a 30 per cent chance of buying at $5.00 and a 40 per cent chance of buying at $4.00. Then, Decision Rule A follows:

a. Buy in the 4th quarter if the cost in the 3rd quarter is $6.00.

b. Buy in the 3rd quarter if the cost in the 3rd quarter is $5.00 or less.

The probability that (b) will occur is 0.70. Consequently, the probability that (a) will occur is 1.00-0.70 = 0.30. From this we derive the expected value of Decision Rule A.

Expected Cost (Decision Rule A) = 0.40 ($4.00) + 0.30 ($5.00) + 0.30($5.40) = $4.72

Step 3: If the cost in the 2nd quarter is \$4.00, we can do better than this expected cost of \$4.72. Decision Rule B is then:

a. Use Decision Rule A if the cost in the 2nd quarter is \$5.00 or greater.

b. Buy in the 2nd quarter if the cost in the 2nd quarter is \$4.00.

The probability that (b) will occur is 0.30. Hence:

Expected Cost (Decision Rule B) = 0.30 (54.00) + 0.70 (\$4.72)
= \$4.504.

Step 4. If the cost in the 1st quarter is \$4.00, we can do better than this expected cost of \$4.504. Decision Rule C follows:

a. Use Decision Rule B if the cost in the 1st quarter is \$5.00 or greater.

b. Buy in the 1st quarter if the cost in the 1st quarter is \$4.00.

The probability that (b) will occur is 0.40. Thus:

Expected Cost (Decision Rule C) = 0.40 (\$4.00) + 0.60 (\$4.504) = \$4.3024.

We have deduced an optimal policy which has an expected cost of \$4.3026.

The importance of commodity buying as one form of procurement has induced us to present a commodity buying model. Inventory levels are strongly affected by such buying decisions. It is important that the student of production management be aware of the elements involved in this vital purchasing situation.

Bidding

Usually, the purchase of fabricated units and components tends to involve more stable price structures than apply to commodities. An organization contract with a producer to supply a given number of units of some specific quality. Under some circumstances, the contract may be given on the basis of bids which are offered by potential vendors. The bid system is commonly associated with governmental acquisition of materials. It is also familiar in situations where industrial organizations have no prior vendor arrangements and in which substantial acquisitions are to be made. It is only useful when a competitive market exists for the items to be acquired.

From the biddy's point of view, there is a probability of winning a supply contract is affected by the number of bidders participating in the bidding competition. In general, as the number of bidders increases, the winning bid will be lower. The reason is that different costing systems, capacity and load conditions, skills and facilities, exist for each bidder. As a result, the range of bids will increase. Based on this reasoning, the procurement manager would seemingly want as many bidders as possible. But there is an opposing force at work. As the number of bidders increases, the cost of ordering rises since each bid must be evaluated, not only for costs but for the many intangible factors that must affect the ordering decision. Perhaps, for example, the lowest bidder will promise to meet a delivery schedule which evaluation indicates is unlikely to be fulfilled.

A company does not, of necessity, choose to make its purchases from the organization presenting the lowest bid. Price is seldom the only factor that should be taken into consideration when awarding a contract. Among other things, it is necessary to consider the guarantees of quality, the experience of the vendor, the certainties of delivery, and the kind of long-term supplier-producer relationship that is likely to develop. Transportation costs further complicate the picture. A high bid received from a vendor that is two miles away may be less costly- after transportation- than a lower bid from a potential supplier located 3000 miles away. Thus, it is not enough to compare bids on an FOB point of origin basis.

The purchasing function is immersed in a maelstrom of human relations. There are many mechanical aspects to the achievement of a successful purchasing function, but the human factors cannot be overlooked. Buyers can succeed in achieving special arrangements because of friendly relationships that exist. These are not dishonorable relationships because they include the evaluation of both buyer and vendor of the long-term stability and goodwill of their relationship.Thus, in the business environment of North America, personal friendships are not considered to be a reasonable basis for enterprise decisions. In other business environments, for exampl, Latin America and The Middle East, personal friendships are considered to be business assets that reduce risk and have monetary value.

Part of this cultural difference can be traced to the importance placed upon legal contracts in North America that does not exist everywhere in the world. Because of the enormous growth of international operations, these factors can play a significant role in determining the success of production management in handling the affairs of subsidiaries outside the USA.

Maintenance inventories

Previously, we mentioned inventories that are primarily maintenance inventories. Consider, for example, an oil refinery: For lack of a few critical parts an entire refinery can be shut down. The cost of lost production may well run into millions of dollars. Should all parts be kept in stock? If so, how many of each kind? How likely is it that a spare part kept in stock for an emergency is, in fact, a reject—a faulty part-that will fail immediately upon use? There are many different kinds of problems that are faced by purchasing agents for maintenance parts. Often, severe technical problems are involved in purchasing for the maintenance function of complex technological systems.

Maintenance parts buyers, in particular, must be familiar with production equipment and its requirements. They must also be able to evaluate the quality of the merchandise they acquire. A rational plan should be developed for purchasing and stocking such items. Maintenance inventory policies are a function of the type of maintenance that is used, that is, preventative or remedial maintenance or a combination of the two. In many systems, the technical basis used for purchasing decisions can be exceedingly critical. When reliability and failure are of major importance, the purchasing function is frequently assigned to a scientifically trained individual. This is particularly necessary when critical specifications are couched in engineering terminology.

A decision model for maintenance inventories

An important class of maintenance inventories is identified with the fact that at the time a major facility is purchased, spare parts can be obtained inexpensively. Later on, however, if it turns out that an insufficient supply of spare parts was acquired, the cost of obtaining additional spares is much higher.

To illustrate, assume that a large punch press has a part which engineering data indicate has a probability of i failures, (pi), over the lifetime of the machine. There is a cost, c, for each spare part purchased at the time that the press is acquired. When a spare part must be purchased at a later time, because not enough were originally purchased, the cost is estimated to be C_u.

For a simple example of this model, let i=1,2,3 meaning that only three failure can occur over the lifetime of the punch press. Also, assume that the probability of 1,2 or 3 failure is equally likely, i.e., $p_1=p_2=p_3=½$. Further, let c=\$5 and C_u=\$40. The question we wish to answer is: How many spare parts, k, should be ordered at the time of the original purchase? A decision matrix can be constructed to represent this problem. Thus:

The outcome entires in the matrix are computed by two different relationships. First, when the number of failures equals or is less than the number of parts originally ordered with the press, the cost is simply *kc*. Second, when the number of failures is greater than the number of parts originally ordered, the cost is $kc+(i-k)C_u$. For example if three failures occur (i=3) and only two parts were originally ordered (k=2), then the cost is (2x5)+(3-2) 40 = 50. After the matrix of total costs is completed, the expected values are obtained in the usual fashion. In our example, the optimal strategy is to order three spare parts with the press. Clearly, the decision matrix lends itself nicely to representing this static form of inventory problem.

Classification of inventory systems

There are many significant distinctions between types of inventories that need to be made. First, let us note, there are items which are functionally critical to operations, no matter how much or how little they cost. For example, the lack of some small spare engine part could ground a 747 aircraft. The need for a cheap pump part might severely slow down a refinery.

Second, there are items that are important because their dollar volume is high. A significant division of all items under materials management is based on the recognition that some few items have high dollar volumes and many others have substantially lower dollar volumes.

Since dollar volume relates directly to

inventory costs, potential savings available as a result of better inventory policies will be far greater in this A class than in any other. This is particularly apparent when it is pointed out that the cost of inventory studies tend to be proportional to the number of items under consideration. The B class (another 25 per cent of all items) may account for another 15 or 20 percent of dollar volume. The C class often deals with no more than 5 to 10 per cent of the company's total dollar volume although 50 per cent of all items inventoried belong in that group. There is no commitment to provide class breaks at 25 and 50 per cent nor a need to abide by three classes. It is essential, however, that the production manager recognize the unequal contributions of different items in his inventory, and the fact that equivalent effort should not be spent on improving the inventory policies of all items.

Another important classification is based on the difference between state and dynamic situations. In the static case, only one inventory decision can be made. The spare parts model is a static case. A well-known problem that is often cited to explain the static situation is the "Christmas tree problem". The man selling Christmas trees can only place a single order for trees. Then, on Christmas day, he finds out whether he estimated exactly right, or guessed over or under. In the case of overestimated demand, salvage value is sometimes available. For example, a department store that overbuys on toys, shipped from abroad in time for the holiday season, can often sell those toys at a discount after the selling season is finished. Dynamic situations do not require this same considerations because the demad for such items is continuous. The problem, as well shall see, becomes one of adjusting inventory levels so as to balance the various costs that apply.

Inventory costs

The heart of inventory analysis resides in the identification of relevant costs. There are many kinds of cost that apply to the inventory situation. We shall now itemize some of those that are most frequently encountered.

1. *Cost of Ordering*: Each time a purchase requisition is drawn up, both fixed and variable costs are incurred. The fixed costs of ordering are associated with the salaries of the permanent staff of the order department. We also include investments in equipment and properly assigned overhead charges. Fixed costs are not affected by the inventory policies that are followed. The variable cost component consists of the purchase requisition form, the cost of sending this purchase requisition to the vendor; in fact, any costs that increase as the number of purchase requisitions increase. Not to be overlooked are opportunity costs associated with alternative uses of both time and equipment. Thus, the ordering cost of a self-employed shopkeeper must take into account that fact that he could be redecorating

his windows, talking longer with a customer, or using his time in some other fruitful manner.

Then, by definition, as the number of orders increases, the fixed costs remain constant; the variable costs increase. For example, a company may be able to process 100 orders per week. If a new inventory policy requires that 150 purchase requisitions-on the average-be processed in a week, then the order in labour costs and equipment and overhead is considered to be additional variable cost. In this way the ordering cost is determined on top of a base ordering system.

2. *The Cost of Carrying Inventory:* It is well known that manufacturers prefer to maintain minimum inventories. We frequently hear that in times of uncertainty companies begin to cut back on their inventory. Why is this so? The answer is that a company maintains an investment in the form of inventory. Their capital is tied up in materials and goods. If the capital were free, alternative uses might be found for it. For example, the company could take this freed capital and put it in the savings bank, thereby earning interest on the money. On the other hand, somewhat more speculative investment could be made in stocks. The company could purchase additional equipment and expand capacity, or even use this money to diversify. Thus, we see that an opportunity cost exists. By holding inventory

the company foregoes investing their capital in alternative ways.

Inventory carrying costs must also include the expense of storing inventory. As was the case for the ordering department, costs should be measured from a fixed base. We must only consider the variable cost component associated with storage—the costs over which the production manager can exercise control in terms of the inventory policies. Thus, if a company has shelf space for 1000 units but can get a discount if they stock a maximum of 2000 units, then to get this discount they must expand their storage capacity, or rent additional space. An appropriate inventory cost analysis must be made to determine whether or not the discount should be taken. The extra costs incurred are a variable cost component associated with holding inventory. It should be noted that the interest charges discussed above are a variable cost which depend upon the number of units stocked, the price per unit, and the interest rate that is determined to be applicable.

Items which are carried in stock are subject to pilferage losses, obsolescence, and deterioration. These costs represent real losses in the volume of inventory. Pilferage is particularly characteristic of certain items. Small items, for example are more likely to disappear than large ones. Tool cribs are provided with attendants and frequently kept locked when the plant is shut down for the single and over the weekend. Tools have general appeal and almost universal utility. They are small enough to filch, ergo, the tool crib concept.

Obsolescence can occur quite suddenly because of technological change. Or it can be the kind of loss that is associated with style goods, toys, and Christmas trees. Out of seasons and out of style, these items lose value and must be sold at a special reduced rate. The problem of determining how much inventory to carry will be affected by the nature of the inventories and the way in which units lose value over time. An additional component of the holding cost includes both taxes and insurance. If insurance rates and taxes are determined on a per unit basis then the amount of inventory that is stocked will determine directly the insurance and tax components of the carrying costs.

As a guide, we can furnish the following table. Hypothetical figures have been entered which are similar to the carrying cost computations of many companies in the USA. Each situation is different and the production manager must assess those costs that apply to his situation.

A sample determination of carrying cost

Loss due to inability to invest funds in profit-making ventures, including loss of interest	14.00
Obsolescence	3.00
Deterioration	3.00
Transportation, handling and distribution	2.00
Taxes	0.25
Storage cost	0.25
Insurance	0.25

General supplies 0.25

Pilferage 0.25

C_c = carrying cost expressed as percent per year = 23.00

3. *Cost of Out of Stock.* If a company cannot fill an order there is usually some penalty to be paid. Sometimes, the customer goes elsewhere, and the penalty is the value of the order that is lost. If the customer is annoyed because he had to do without or find a new supplier and he continues to hold a grudge against the company, then the loss of a sale plus the loss of goodwill number translated into a cost. If the buyer is willing to wait to have his order filled, then the company treats this situation as a back order. Back orders cost money. They can annoy the customer even though he appears to be willing to wait. Many times, a company will attempt to fill the customer's order with a more expensive substitute. The cost factor is not difficult to determine in this case. Whatever the system: Fill or kill, back ordering, material substitutions, and so on, some costs of being out of stock will occur. The lost goodwill cost is considered to be one of the most significant and one of the most difficult to evaluate.

4. *Other Costs.* The above named costs are the ones that usually are considered most relevant in the determination of inventory policy. Many other costs also play a part in specific cases. Thus, for example, there are systemic costs associated with running the inventory system,

costs of delays in processing orders, costs of discounts not realized, setup costs, costs of production interruptions, salvage costs, and expenditing costs. In some instances, one or more of these costs will dominant the inventory policy evaluation.

Economic-order-quantity model

Now let us see how these costs operate in an inventory system and the way in which they can be balanced so that an optimal inventory procedure is followed. We will treat a dynamic system under certainty where no stock outages are allowed to occur. By dynamic we mean that inventory does not lose value after a given date, such as Christmas, and that a continuing demand will exist over the long run.

Now let us consider the policy of ordering twice a year. There would be 250 units ordered with each of two purchase requisitions. These 250 units get used up gradually until nothing is left. At that point, the next order of 250 units arrives. The stock level shoots back up to a full bin of 250 units. Then the decline begins again until, at the end of the year, nothing is left and another new shipment will be immediately received. We now have half of the 250 units as the measure of the average number of units of inventory, viz., 125 units. The ordering cost is incurred twice but the carrying cost is applied to the smaller average inventory of only 125 units. Figure illustrates this, and it also shows what would happen with five orders per year. Each purchase requisition consists of a request for 100 units. The average number of units on hand would now be 50, and the variable cost per order is incurred five times.

In each case the total variable cost is the sum of the total variable ordering cost component and the total variable carrying cost component. Thus:

Total Cost = Total Variable Carrying Cost + Total Variable Ordering Cost

The basis of inventory theory is to write an appropriate cost equation including all possible costs, such as obsolescence, pilferage, and so on, if they apply. Then we proceed to minimize this total cost equation. It is quite clear that different costs results from different ordering policies. The smallest possible carrying charges would occur when we placed 500 orders for one unit apiece. On the other hand, a very small ordering cost could be achieved by ordering very infrequently, say once every five years.

It is the sum of the two cost factors, ordering cost B and carrying cost A. This equation has a minimum, that is, total cost is minimized when $x=x_o$.

Economic lot size model

Having investigated the relationship that describes the optimal order quantity when purchase orders are placed with an outside vendor, let us now consider the comparable problem—identical in all respects except that the company is its own supplier. We call this formulation the economic lot-size model, ELS, because the production run quantity is called a "lot". The sharp, saw-tooth form that applied to the EOQ case, where a total shipment of stock was received at one point in time, has been replaced by a gradual stock build-up. The rate of decline would be equivalent in both situations. In this case, x_o is the optimal run size. The cost of an order is no longer relevant. In its place we substitute C_2, which is the setup cost which is usually much larger than the order cost. Then, all other things being equal, we expect that the optimal run size would be largest than the optimal order size. The setup cost is composed of at least two parts (1) The cost of labor required to prepare the facility for the new production run and (2) The cost of lost production occasioned by the facility being down while being prepared for the new job. In addition, we shall name two other variables:

p = production rate in units per day

d = demand rate in units per day.

The optimal run size is derives in a manner similar to the derivation of the economic order quantity, with the following result.

$$x_0 = \sqrt{\frac{2zC_s}{cC_c}\left(\frac{p}{p-d}\right)}$$

If *d* is almost equal to p, then x_o becomes very large, approaching infinity at the difference between d and p approaches zero. This result makes sense. In effect it states: If the demand rate is as great as the production rate, then run the process continuously. On the other hand, if p is very much greater than d, that is, p>>>d, then x_o

equals EOQ. This result is also reasonable. The condition that is given approximates the state of being able to receive total replenishment upon request.

As an example of the ELS model, let us use the following numbers:

z = 1000 parts per year = 4 parts per day

C_2 = \$200 per setup

c = \$5 per part

C_c = 0.10 per dollar per year

p = 5 parts per day = 1250 parts per year

d = 4 parts per day = 1000 parts per year

Lead time

For both economic order quantity and the economic lot size systems, the lead time required to supply items for inventory must be known. In Figure the lead time or replenishment time is called LT.

Consider the EOQ case. The obvious components of lead time include the period for recognition of the fact that it is time to reorder; the interval for doing whatever clerical work in needed; mail or telephone intervals for communicating with the vendor; then, recognition of the order by the vendor who will see whether the requested items are in stock, and if not, will set up to make them. Next, the vendor ships the items, so there is delivery time. The items are delivered but must be processed by the receiving department which may require inspection. Until the items are entered on the warehouse stock cards, the lead time continues. Similar descriptions could be given for the ELS case, where the sometimes illusory advantages of dealing within your own firm, and thereby having greater control, appear.

It should be noted, that when the job shop configuration exists, the EOQ model can be applied to self-supply with batch production. Figure helps to illustrate why this is so.

Quantity-discount model

If a quantity discount is offered, should it be taken? When does the discount potential override the selection of the optimal undiscounted order quantity x_o? By using sets of total-cost equations, it is possible to analyze whether or not a quantity discount that is offered should cancel out the x_o value associated with the undiscounted minimum total cost.

The discounting situation is directly reflected by the following schedule:

The top curve TC(c) is based on an undiscounted cost, c. The bottom curve TC(c') is applicable when a discount is available, but it is only applicable at and above the quantity needed to obtain the discount. Let x, be the specified quantity required to obtain the discount. If x_j, is x_1 in Figure, then the discount must be taken. In fact the order quantity should be increased from x_1 to x_b which intersects point b. Point b is the minimum total cost that can be obtained in the discount region. Note, the top curve applies from

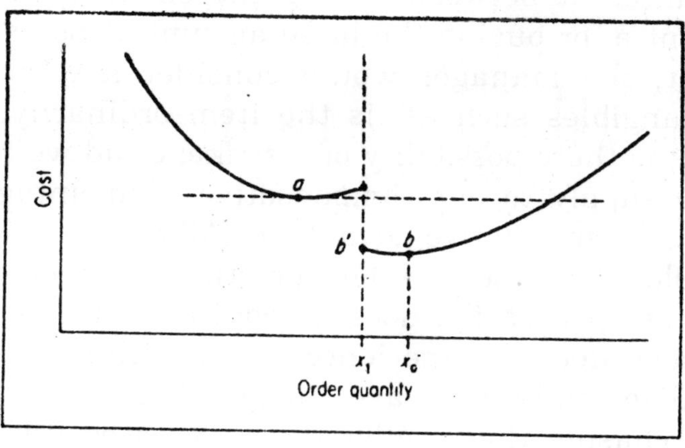

$x=0$ to $x<x_1$; the bottom curve applies for $x \geq x_1$. Figure illustrates this discontinuity. The cost of point b is lower than that of point b'. Returning to Figure, when x_1 is specified at x_2, then point c provides a lower cost then point a. Point a is the minimum total cost without the discount. Point c is the lowest total cost that is available in the discount region. So x_2 units should be purchased. Again referring to figure, if $x_j = x_3$, the intersected cost point is e which is a greater cost than a. Therefore, the order quantity corresponding to point a should be used. The same reasoning can be extended to more than one price

break for quantity discounts and a purely mathematical approach can be used as well. If the quantity specified for discount intersected point d, the manager (theoretically) would be indifferent between buying the small amount at point a, or buying the large amount at point d. In fact, the manager would consider a variety of intangibles such as :is the item ordinarily hard get; is there possibility of a strike; could we corner the supply to our compensative advantage? Is there a speculative advantage? All of these notions could favor point d. On the other hand, does this items spoil easily, does it require a lot of storage space, does it experience a high pilferage rate? These thoughts are more likely to favor purchasing the smaller quantity associated with point a.

Multiple items and aggregate inventories

Inventories are seldom composed of a single item. Usually, many different items are carried in stock. Even for a signal items, it is not unusual to many associated stockkeeping units. For example, in the category "screws" a typical manufacturers inventory will include various diameters, number of threads to the inch, wood screws, machine screws, philips head screws, brass screws steel screws, and so on. In the same way, a department store will carry many different sizes, colours, materials, and styles of such and supermarket stocks a great variety of soups and soaps.

We could, if we had enough formation, obtain the optimal order quantity or lot size for each

S K U. This would give us the minimum overall total system. However, two factors intervene.

1. It costs money to study inventories and to develop polices for each S K U. From the point of view of a break even chart, the cost of the inventory study increases fixed costs. The savings obtained from the study decrease able costs. The resultant must represent a sufficient return on the capital invested in the inventory study to make this investment preferable to alternative investments in bonds and stocks, machinery, or additional persons. Because this criterion underlies all inventory studies, companies seldom undertake inventory studies of all the items that are needed. Instead, as previously discussed the Items are divided into categories—frequently called A-B-C.

2. The company's resources are limited. It is frequently unreasonable to carry the total average dollar inventory that the individual items' optimal policies would require. The capacity of the ordering department may be over taxed; storage facilities may be filled to capacity; the amount of capital invested in inventory may exceed the amount that the company has available. These limitations, if they exist, require a modification of inventory policy. That is, the theoretical system's optimal is not feasible because it violates other practical system's constraints

Let us first relax the requirement with respect to unlimited capital resources. We will assume that company policy calls for no more than \$2000 to be invested in inventory, on the average. But the sum of the optimal policies for each product requires a total average inventory investment of \$2600. What then should be done? The cash limit prevents the use of the individual items' optimal inventory policies. The figures for this example are given below, where $C_c = 0.24$ per year and $C_r = \$48.00$ per order.

Let A = Total average dollar inventory, and

a_j = Average dollar inventory of the jth item, which has a per unit cost of c_j a yearly demand of z_j and an optimal orderquantity of x_o.

Then, it can readily be shown that for a rational ordering policy:

This important systems oriented equation states that for each item, j, a dollar volume relationship exists with the total dollar volume of all items held in inventory. Defying ordinary intuition, the proportionality is in terms of square roots. That is, the square root of j's dollar volume in ratio with the sum of the square roots of all items, including j, specefies the appropriate average dollar investment in j's inventory as a part of the total dollar inventory for all items. We should note that A is not required to be an optimal value. It is usually set by arbitrary policy. Managerial intitution can hardly be faulted if it finds square root proportions of part to the whole difficult to drive. This is especially true after noting that A can be set in an arbitrary fashion. In many companies the value of A is handed down by top management according to its perception of prevailing economic and social conditions and changed without warning from time to time.

Let us derive the necessary values for our example, letter A=$2000 as specified.

We can now recompute the rational order quantities directly.

This problem is resolved. We should order 307 units of item 1 instead of the optimal order quantity of 400. Similarly, order 769 units of item 2 instead of 100 units; order 770 units of item 3 instead of 1000 units; and order 308 units of item 4 instead of 400 units.

The same kind of thinking can be applied to the number of orders that are placed assuming that no constraint exists for A.

where n_j represents the number of orders to be placed for the jth, items and N stands for the total number of orders that can be made by the order department. This formulation is used when there is an upper limit to the capacity of the ordering department.

The reason that the multiple item inventory policies that we have just described are rational—as compared to other policies that would be irrational is based on two points.

1. It is not irrational to find oneself unable to achieve the system's over-all optimal state

because resource limitations make it impossible to operate at this over-all optimal level.

2. The existence of constraints of one kind or another, if they prohibit the use of the over-all optimal policy, imply the fact that the costs, C and C_r, that have been used to determine the over-all optimal policy, cannot both be correct measures of the situation. Therefore, a rational policy is one where an appropriate change in these costs would provide an optimal policy that would meet the constraints. This is what the above formulation succeeds in doing.

Perpetual inventory systems

The economic lot-size model and the economic order-quantity model are based on the assumption that there will be no variability in demand. In most practical instances this assumption cannot be sustained. As a result, a class of inventory models has been designed to cope with situations where the demand level fluctuates.

Many companies use perpetual inventory systems wherein withdrawal quantities are entered on the item's stock card each and every time that a unit is withdrawn from stock. The withdrawal quantity is subtracted from the previous stock level to determine the present quantity of stock on hand. A minimum level is designated as the reorder level for each item. This reorder point quantity is marked on the respective stock card. When the minimum level has been reached, then an order is placed for the economic order quantity, x_o. The level of stock represented by the reorder point is equal to the expected demand in the lead time, plus what is called the reserve stock or buffer stock. This buffer has been designed to absorb a certain percentage of the fluctuations in demand that are likely to occur for each particular item. The reserve stock is geared to provide some chosen level of protection against stock outages. The level that is chosen is based on the balance of out-of-stock costs and carrying costs associated with the reserve stock.

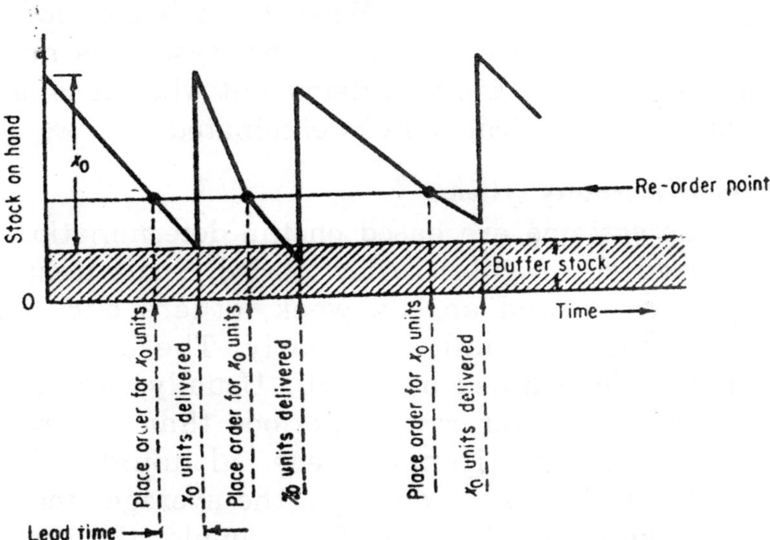

The calculation of the reorder point is not difficult to accomplish. First, to has been noted, stock must be provided to cover the expected demand in the lead time period. Call this S. Then additional buffer stock is to be provided which gives some specified level of protection against going out of stock in the same lead time interval. Call this additional inventory B. The above figure depicts the situation for a probability distribution of demand in the lead time period.

The so-called two-bin system provides a clever way of continuously monitoring the reorder point in a perpetual inventory system. Figure is almost self-explanatory in this regard.

When a replenishment order is received, Bin 1 is filled to the reorder point level. The remainder of the order is placed in Bin 2. Obviously, if Bin 1 is at the reorder point level, all of the incoming items are placed in Bin 2. When Bin 2 is emptied, a new order is placed. The two bin system is not feasible for many kinds of items, but when it is, a great deal of clerical work is eliminated.

Periodic inventory systems

Periodic systems are based on the determination of a fixed and regular review period. Some items may be reviewed once a week, others once a month, semi-annually, or yearly. The optimal period is determined by $x_0/z=t_0$. Usually, certain items have shorter review periods than others. These would be items where, although the demand level is relatively high, the average stock level is kept low, because, for example, the cost per unit is high. At each review, the stock on hand is determined. An order is then placed for a variable quantity. This quantity is larger than usual when demand has been greater than expectation. It is smaller than usual when demand has been less than expectation. Thus, in the case of the periodic inventory model, the review period is fixed, but the order quantity is variable.

The target level M is determined by calculating the expected demanding review period plus one lead time interval. To this is added buffer stock which offers protection against excessive demand in a review period plus one and time interval. In fact, when the optimal order quantity x_o is subracted from the target level M, the stock remaining has an expected value equivalent to the reorder point of the perpetual inventory model. On the other hand, the clerical costs of the perpetual model are higher than those of the period model. The clerical cost advantage of the periodic model disappears, however, when on-line, real-time computer system operate the perpetual model's calculation requirements. As a result, there is a distinct trend toward perpetual systems and away from periodic ones.

Value analysis

Of relatively recent origin, the concept of value analysis has been widely accepted by industry. The fundamental notion of value analysis is that the quality of the production output must be maintained while at the same time the cost of the output should be decreased. Although value analysis is applied to all phases of the production process, in practice, it emphasizes the selection of the input materials. If this were not the case, it would be hard to distinguish value analysis from traditional methods analysis which is, according to its own title, dedicated to the study and improvement of production methods. It is inevitable that value and methods analysis must share some common ground, tackle the same kind of problems, and provide essentially the same kind of problem resolution. Undoubtedly, the recent surge of interest in value analysis can be explained, at least in part, by the fact that materials technology has been undergoing rapid and dramatic changes. New materials are constraint being made available through research efforts.

For the most part, the procedures of value analysis are applied to established products rather than to new ones. The essence of value analysis is embodied in the high degree of organization of the approach. This is evidenced by a structured set of relevant questions. For example:

1. What is this item intended to do?
2. How much does it cost to make this item?
3. What else could do the same job?
4. How much does the suggested alternative cost?

The taxonomy of quality, reveals that the problems of defining what an item is intended to do are enormously complex and not well understood. Accordingly, the utility of value analysis will be dependent upon the knowledge and creative insight that the individuals who are doing these studies can bring to bear. The value analysis approach has been designed to release such insights by providing a structural framework to encourage the development of alternative strategies. The procedural starting point is the examination of an existing output. The purposes or functions of this output are divided into primary and secondary classes. Significant functions are then related by analogy to other items and then to materials which are thought to provide similar properties.

It is through the analogic method that value alternatives are derived. Thus, for example, we might develop comparisons between different joining methods which include adhesion, cohesion, welding, brazing, and mechanical fastenings such as screws, nuts and bolts, lock washers, cotter pins, and nails. Harking back to decision theory, we find that both methods analysis and value analysis are primarily intended as a means for discovering new tactical alternatives. Any approach that succeeds in improving this aspect of decision making is of real importance when properly used. But we must always guard against investments in efficiency studies before effectiveness issues have been thoroughly considered.

Job shop materials control

In the job shop, inventory controls are often based on fulfilling a schedule in line with an outside contract or internal orders placed by other departments. The inventory models previously discussed are less well-suited to this task than are the kinds of controls developed for network models of projects.

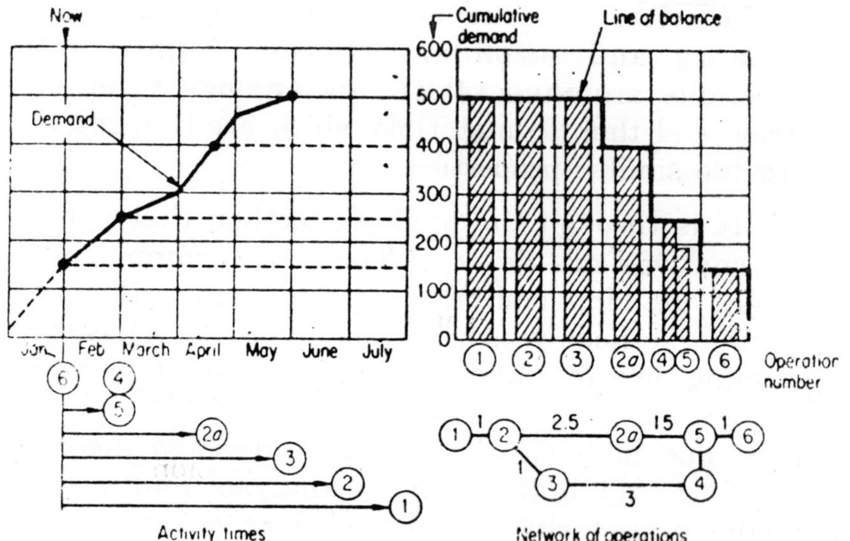

The Conventional LOB Graph

On the other hand, the extensive complexity of the project networks differs from that of the job shop system where many jobs that are independent of each other must be kept track of simultaneously. The line of balance (LOB) technique is quite well-suited to this situation. As in the critical path system this approach begins with a network of activities and events. The LOB network uses the completion or delivery of readily identifiable part components as these events. The activities between the event nodes are processing and assembly operation.

A graph of cumulative production as promised by contract is drawn with respect to calendar time. It should be noted that cumulative production is measured as end-product units. Therefore, if two parts are needed in a unit, that fact is taken into account in the interpretation of the charts. Present time is located on the graph and with it is associated the final event node of the network. All other network nodes are measured from that node, and located at their proper place in time. Where the time line of each event intersects the cumulative shipment curve is the appropriate inventory level for the part having the specific event number. These points are called the line of balance. The LOB describes the stock level that should have been satisfied for the part in question.

2 Materials Management

Introduction

If the manufacturing, trading, and profit and loss account of any British manufacturing business is examined it is likely that a large proportion of all costs incurred during a period can be attributed to the requisition and storage of materials and components. Also, from an examination of the balance sheet, a large proportion of funds invested in the business's working capital is likely to be found invested in stocks of raw materials and components. These two observations have not gone unnoticed by business owners and managers who have concentrated their resources on devising ways of organising their firms with the objective of controlling the purchasing and storage of materials and components. The effects of poor buying and bad stock control are increased costs and inefficiency. This chapter looks at the ways business can be organised to ensure that the purchasing and storage functions are carried out efficiently and with the minimum of cost. It also takes a brief overview of the whole production function and the relationship between the departments comprising that function.

Materials management is the name given to the modern approach it purchasing and stock management, it integrates both the purchasing and stock management functions, enabling the firm to benefit from a close liaison between the stores personnel and the buyers. The integrated materials function is managed by a *materials manager*, who is responsible for both the stores and purchasing.

The organisation of the materials function

In many business the materials function is structured as part of the production function, the materials manager being responsible to the *production director or production manager*. This is the traditional organisation of purchasing and stock and is based on the premise that the acquisition of materials and stores are both part of the production function. In practice, materials consumed by a business are influenced by both sales forecasts and the production budget, as there is an interdependence between demand and supply. To recognise the relationship between marketing, production and materials management, a number of firms are now organising their materials function as separate from their production function, the materials manager being responsible to the board of directors. Such a structure recognises that the rate of consumption of materials depends ultimately upon demand.

The responsibilities of the materials manager

The responsibilities of the materials manager are likely to include:

(a) the purchasing of raw materials and components;

(b) the running of the stores and maintenance of stock levels;

(c) participating in product and process design on a consulting basis;

(d) keeping up to date with the development and introduction of raw materials;

(e) providing information for use in the preparation of a purchasing budget.

Purchasing

The objectives of the purchasing department

The objectives of the purchasing department should be to ensure that materials are purchased:

(a) at the right price;

(b) from the best supplier;

(c) of the right quality;

(d) in the right quantity;

(e) at the right time.

The right price

A firm's costs will be minimised only when materials are purchased at their optimal price. This will be the lowest price for which materials can be purchased that satisfies all the other objectives of purchasing. Consideration must be given to bulk discounts, other discounts and credit terms.

The best supplier

Features such as reliability, efficiency at dealing with queries and after-sales service vary from supplier to supplier. The supplier offering the best service that complies with the needs of the purchasing firm should be used. The best supplier will only be found by the buyer using his experience and knowledge of the trade.

The right quality

All materials bought for use in production should comply with the product specification. If they are below standard then can have far-reaching effects on production costs and profits of the firm. The use of substandard materials can result in:

(i) spoilt production;

(ii) high wastage of materials;

(iii) inefficient use of labour;

(iv) increased machine time needed by production;

(v) increased wear on machines.

All of these problems will increase costs and reduce production efficiency. The purchase of materials that are of a better standard than needed may result in a higher price being paid for them, although this may be compensated by other costs being saved because of increased efficiency resulting from their use.

In the right quantity

Materials should be purchased in sufficient quantities to minimise the risk of running our of stock, minimise purchasing costs and keep storage costs to a minimum. Purchase quantities can be controlled by employing stock-control techniques that calculate an optimal order quantity.

At the right time

Materials should be purchased so that they will be delivered when they re needed. If they are bought too early then excessive storage costs will be incurred. If they are bought too late then the firm may run out of materials with the result that production is interrupted.

The objectives of purchasing should be related to the objectives of each business, co-ordinated with the other functions and expressed in detail as its *purchasing policy*.

The function of the purchasing department

The primary function of the purchasing department is to carry out management policy relating to the purchase of raw materials, components, stores and equipment. The purchasing department is likely to have only limited authority expenditure. Most business establish an upper limit for expenditure and allow only specific types of purchases to be carried out by the purchasing department. Materials and components are usually included but authorisation for the purchase of expensive capital equipment is not normally given to the purchasing department, and is normally only sanctioned by senior management. The duties of the purchasing department should include the following.

Carrying out the purchasing procedure

Every business should have a purchasing procedure that is followed whenever a purchase of material is made. A typical procedure is as follows:

(i) A purchase requisition is completed by the appropriate department, e.g. stores, ad is authorised by a person holding the recognised responsibility, e.g. chief storekeeper.

(ii) The authorised purchase requisition is then passed to the purchasing department. A buyer then selects a supplier from the list of accredited suppliers or seeks a quotation from a number of accredited suppliers. Prices and terms are then negotiated and an order is then made out and placed with the best supplier. Orders made by telephone should be confirmed in writing.

(iii) Once an order has been placed with a supplier it should be monitored and if necessary chased up to ensure the delivery of materials is made on time.

(iv) When materials are received they should be checked with the delivery note and the order to ensure that they are as ordered and in the correct quantity. In delivered balances should be recorded as still outstanding. On acceptance of the materials the goods should be recorded in the materials inwards records.

Payment

The purchasing department should agree final acceptance of materials received and that they are as ordered. If they are satisfactory then authorisation should be made for payment to the supplier.

Market intelligence

The purchasing department should keep up to date with new development concerning materials and components available, suppliers and markets. Price trends and forecasts should be studied and projected into the future. Economic factors influencing the market should be studied, e.g. takeover or mergers of suppliers. Businesses whose raw materials suffer from wide fluctuations of price often make purchases in the "future" markets of their raw materials. This means they agree to purchase a specific quantity of a commodity at an agreed price at a fixed future date. The objective of this is to beat anticipated price rises in their raw materials. Future buying is highly speculative and requires considerable expertise on the part of the buyer.

Supplier appraisal

Whenever alternative suppliers exist for materials then each supplier should be evaluated by the purchasing department and a list of accredited suppliers produced. Suppliers listed as accredited are those which meet the standards of the purchasing firms.

A business should not place itself in a position where it is wholly dependent on only one supplier—material suppliers should be encouraged to compete for business. The accredited list of suppliers should be compiled on the basis of buyers' knowledge of suppliers and their experience in the market. It should be regularly reviewed to ensure it is up to date, changes being made whenever necessary.

Purchasing research

Purchasing research is an important activity of the purchasing department. The person responsible for purchasing research should research into:

Suppliers

A researcher should find out what alternative suppliers exist for each material or component and the terms of trade offered by each. Particular attention should be taken in finding out when new suppliers enter a market and who they are. Contact should be made with them as soon as possible. Researchers should also find to as soon as possible if and when existing suppliers are planning to withdraw from a market or discontinue a product line.

Prices

Research should be made into prices to ensure that up-to-date information on price is readily available. Price forecasts should be made so that information is available that can be used in the preparation of budgets and so that the firm can exploit expected falls in prices and minimize the effects of anticipated price rises, e.g. by purchasing additional stocks before a price rise.

Materials

Research into the alternative materials that are available will provide information that can be passed on to the production design and planing and control departments. In formation can also be passed on about new materials as soon as it is known.

The organisation of the purchasing function

As with the other functions of a business, the way in which the purchasing function will be organised depends to a large extent on the size and nature of the business. In smaller firms the number of employees engaged in purchasing will be relatively few, in such cases one person will be responsible for performing many duties. In large, complex organisations, large, extensive purchasing departments may exist, each person employed within the department specializing in only a limited range of activities. Alternative ways of organising the purchasing function are:

Centralized purchasing

When a business organizes its purchasing function centrally only one purchasing department is established. This is located centrally and is responsible for making purchases for the whole organisation. Centralization of purchasing enables economies to be made such as large quantity discounts to be taken advantage of and fewer orders being made. But local knowledge of suppliers will not be available. Smaller businesses with only a small purchasing department are likely to have a centralized purchasing function, as it will be uneconomic to have a number of smaller decentralized departments.

Decentralised purchasing

When a business separates the purchasing function into a number of separately organised divisions, each division is autonomous and is responsible for purchases made within its sphere of operations. An example of decentralised purchasing is when a business is divided into geographical regions, each region with its own purchasing department. A business that organizes its purchasing function in this way will benefit by local knowledge being available. An alternative structure would be to divide the purchasing function into autonomous divisions, each of which is responsible for a group of materials. This would enable each division to acquire and use specialist knowledge and enable the unique characteristics of each group to be known.

A combination of centralized and decentralised purchasing

Many larger firms organize their purchasing function in way in which part is decentralised.

Which of the three alternative methods of organisation a firm uses depends on the size of the firm, the nature of its business and management policy. The one selected and used should be the one from which the from will benefit most.

Materials Control

The objectives of materials control

A large proportion of the working capital of a manufacturing business is likely to be invested in stock. This makes it crucial for management to control stock if working capital is to be efficiently used. If stock is not readily available when required then production will be disrupted, if excessive stock is held then unnecessary costs will be incurred. The objective of stock control can be summarized as follows:

(a) to keep storage costs to a minimum;

(b) to ensure materials are available when required;

(c) to preserve and protect materials in stock, e.g. prevent deterioration, pilferage, waste, loss etc;

(d) to facilitate the planning of material requirements;

(e) to co-operate with user departments;

(f) to keep accurate records and provide information to management relating to stock and stock levels.

The usual method for achieving these objectives is to establish and control a store or stores.

Types of stores

The types of stores used in practice vary from firm to firm and not two stores are likely to be identical. Stores are usually classified by type as follows;

(a) *Raw material stores* in which material stocks are kept.

(b) *Component stores* holding parts used for assembling finished goods or sold outside the business as spare parts.

(c) *Finished-parts stores* in which finished parts are stored ready for final assembly

(e) *Tool store* in which loose tools used in the factory or by service engineers are stored when not in use.

(f) *Maintenance stores* in which spare parts for use in the repair of machinery, cleaning materials and incidentals are stored before they are needed.

(g) *General stores* in which all stock is stored irrespective of its intended use. Small businesses will normally only have a general store and a finished-goods store.

The type of stores a firm uses will depend on such criteria as the nature of the industry, size of the form, methods of production used, factory layout and management policy.

Siting of the stores

The siting of the stores is an important decision, as badly located stores will increase costs unnecessarily and result in loss of production and a drop in efficiency, e.g. causing delays while materials are transported from the stores to the user location. Stores should be conveniently situated to facilitate the efficient receiving of materials inwards and the efficient issue and transport of stock to the user departments. The basic choice for the siting of the stores within the factory complex is largely dependent on how many store are decided upon. Management must make the familiar centralization or decentralisation decision regarding the stores.

Centralization of stores

When this is decided upon the stores are centralized in one location only, thus creating one centrally situated store serving all user departments from the same place. A centralized store has the advantages of:

(i) reducing the physical quantities of stock requiring to be kept, which will result in lower stock holding costs, lower risks of obsolescence and deterioration, less working capital needed, less space needed and lower insurance costs;

(ii) enabling specialist storage facilities to be utilized efficiently, e.g. refrigeration, air-conditioning, storage tanks etc.,

(iii) requiring less staff;

(iv) facilitating easier stock control and stock taking;

(v) reducing the amount of recording necessary

However, there are also a number of disadvantages must be offset. The most important disadvantages are:

(i) time and expense is wasted while the user department obtains stores from a remotely located store;

(ii) internal transport costs will be high;

(iii) the individual needs of specialist user departments may not be catered for;

(iv) the specialist knowledge of user departments

Decentralised stores

An alternative to locating stores centrally is to have a number of separate stores strategically placed around the factory complex, e.g. in each user department. The advantages and disadvantages of decentralised stores are those of centralized stores in reverse, i.e. the advantages of a centralized store are the disadvantage of a decentralised one.

Main store with substores

An alternative to locating stores centrally or decentrally is to have a compromise between the two. This involves having a main store sited centrally with a series of substores strategically located near or in the user departments. This benefits from the advantages of a centralized store while overcoming the disadvantages. The substores obtain stocks from the main store when required and issue them to the user departments.

The stores layout

The design and layout of stores is important as stock should be economically and efficiently stored, i.e. storage costs should be minimized and stock should be stored where it can easily be locate and removed. Stock should also be stored safely with the minimum risk of accident or damage. A well-designed stores layout should include the following features:

(a) heavy goods are stored on the floor:

(b) goods prone to damage from damp are kept in a dry location;

(c) valuable and dangerous materials are kept under secure conditions;

(d) fragile goods are stored in conditions which minimize their risk of being damaged;

(e) materials most frequently issued are stored where they are easily accessible;

(f) inflammable and explosive materials are protected from their inherent risks;

(g) the weight restrictions of the building are strictly complied with;

(h) the use of mechanical aids is facilitated;

(i) related matrials are stored near each other.

Once the stores layout has been designed it must then be equipped. Full advantage should be taken of new developments in stores equipment. Stores equipment includes shelving, racks, bins and handling equipment and may be either:

(a) portable, whereby changes can easily be made; or

(b) fixed, whereby changes can only be made with difficulty and at considerable expense.

Organisation of the stores

The stores are likely to be the responsibility of one person. The title of that person varies from firm to firm, common examples being chief storekeeper, head storeman or stores supervisor. He is normally responsible to the materials manager and he will be expected:

(a) to supervise personnel employed in the stores;

(b) to provide management with information and adviser on matters relating to the stores;

(c) to co-operate with the production, planning, purchasing, inspection and any other departments which use the service provided by the stores;

(d) to maintain a comprehensive, accurate and up-to-date set of stores records;

(e) to ensure an economic and efficient service is provided to user departments;

(f) to issue stock when it is required in compliance with the rules and procedures of the business;

(g) to ensure that physical stocks agree with the stores records;

(h) to check goods received from suppliers against delivery notes nd records and report to the purchasing department any variances.

The stores should be organised in such a way that the stores supervisor and his staff can carry out these duties effectively, efficiently and economically. Small businesses may only have one storekeeper performing all duties, large businesses tend to have one or more store together with an extensive and complex stock system requiring a number of stores personnel. In such a situation responsibilities are frequently organised into division of:

(a) warehouse, responsible for the actual receipt, storage and issue of physical stock;

(b) stores accounts, responsible for the maintenance of stores records;

(c) stock control, responsible for stock levels and stock taking.

Stock control

The objectives of stock control

The main objective of stock control are:

(a) To avoid holding excessive quantities of stock, therefore keeping stock holding costs to a minimum. Holding costs include:

  (i) interest on capital tied up;

  (ii) loss due to deterioration, obsolescence and pilferage of materials;

  (iii) warehouse and handling costs;

  (iv) insurance;

  (v) storekeepers' wages.

(b) To minimize the risk of running out of stock. If a stock-out occurs if frequently causes a production stoppage resulting in productive resources being lost, delay in completing customer order, lost sales and lost customer goodwill.

(c) To minimize the cost of making purchases. Purchasing costs tend to increase as the number of purchaser orders placed with suppliers increases.

An effective stock control system is one that results in these objectives being achieved. A good stock control system requires:

(a) accurate and up-to-date stores records;

(b) regular stock taking;

(c) the establishment of predetermined stock levels.

Stores records

Methods of keeping stores records that assist stock control are:

Two-bin system

This is a well-tried system that consists of two bins for each individual type of stock. One the working bin and the other the reserve bin. The contents of the working bin are issued until it is empty; the storekeeper then commences to issue the contents of the reserve bin which becomes the working bin. when a working bin is emptied the storekeeper advises the purchasing department, which reorders that particular stock them. When the order is delivered it is placed in the empty bin, which then becomes the reserve bin. Stores records are simple and record keeping is kept to a minimum, a bin and for each bin normally being sufficient.

Imprest system

This system of stores records requires a preprinted stock sheet for each individual type of stock noting the stock level. At regular intervals the quantity of each item in stock is recorded and compared with the normal stock level. The difference is noted and the amount in stock is less than the normal stock level then the quantity required is meted in the documents. The stock sheet is then signed, dated and passed to the purchasing department, as a purchase requisition. The imprest system ensures that purchases are based upon current stock levels and requirements. It also keeps stores records to a minimum and where stores are centrally organised acts as a formal purchase requisition procedure.

Reorder level cards

This system of stores records requires a stock card to be kept for each individual type of stock, each card showing a reorder quantity and reorder level. Issues and receipts of stock are posted by the stock clerk who makes out a purchase requisition for the reorder quantity when the reorder level is reached. The purchase requisition is then passed to the chief stock clerk, stores accountant or stores manager for authorization and is then passed to the purchasing department.

Cyclical reordering

This system involves making purchase orders for standard quantities of stock at regular intervals. This method of stores records is simple to operate but can easily result in a stock-out or overstocking. It is only suitable when consumption of a material is constant. The reorder quantity should be based upon forecast consumption during the period between orders and maintaining a buffer stock. A regular review of the standard quantity is necessary and should be amended to meet any expected changes in conditions.

Stock taking

Any system of stock records should be checked at least once a year by comparing physical stocks with the records. The objective of this is to:

(a) ensure the system is reliable and meets the needs of the business;

(b) detect errors and expedite their rectification;

(c) check for pilferage;

(d) provide information on stock quantities and values in management reports, management accounts and financial statements;

(e) identify obsolete and slow-moving stocks.

There are two basic alternative methods of stock taking. They are periodic stock checking and perpetual inventory.

Periodic stock checking

This involves physically checking and counting all stock on the same day at regular intervals, e.g. annually. Results are noted and compared with the stock records. Periodic stock checking, even in a moderately sized business, is a considerable task and requires a lot of organising and effort. Disruption to production frequently occurs during stock checking, as issues from the stores must be restricted while stock checking takes place. To complete the check in the shortest possible time, personnel who are unfamiliar with the store may have to be switched from their normal duties. This will necessitate close supervision throughout the procedure.

Perpetual inventory

This is method of counting and checking stock continuously throughout at period by a relatively few specialist staff who are familiar with the stores. This method should be systematic to ensure that all stock items are checked, counted and the results compared with the stores records at least once during each period. Differences should be reported and investigated where, necessary, stores records being amended to show the correct position. continuous stock checking has a number of advantages over periodic stock checking, including that:

(i) it eliminates the disruption of production;

(ii) errors will be detected sooner;

(iii) it discourages pilferage because it is not known in advance when each stock item is to be checked;

(iv) sow-moving and obsolete stock will be identified earlier;

(v) weaknesses in the system are more likely to be exposed sooner.

Obsolete and slow-moving stock

Slow-moving stock

These should be identified as soon as possible as reorder levels and reorder quantities may have to be reduced and reorder intervals extended, to prevent over-stocking. If slow-moving stock items are allowed to become overstocked:

(i) the risks of obsolescence increase;

(ii) the stock may deteriorate, resulting in unnecessary waste;

(iii) stocks will become excessive, taking up valuable storage space and increasing stock holding costs unnecessarily.

Obsolete stocks

These should be reported as soon as possible and their cause investigated. Good planning and control should avoid the problem of obsolete stock, which is wasteful and costly. Obsolete stock should be disposed of quickly if no alternative use can be found for it. To hold on to it only increases holding costs and takes up storage space by storing useless materials.

Stock levels

To enable a stock control system to effectively achieve its objective a number of predetermined stock levels should be established and maintained for each individual type of stock. These levels are a minimum stock level, maximum stock level, reorder level and an economic order quantity.

Minimum stock level

This is th buffer stock and is the level of stock below which stocks should not normally be allowed to fall. it should take into account:

(i) the reorder level;

(ii) the normal rate of consumption;

(iii) the reorder period.

Maximum stock level

In the level above which stock should not normally be allowed to rise. If stocks do exceed this level excessive holding costs will be incurred. The setting of this level should take into account:

(i) the rate of consumption:

(ii) the time necessary to obtain delivery;

(iii) the reorder quantity;

(iv) the reorder level.

Reorder level

The setting of a reorder level enables control to be exercised over the requisitioning of purchases. It answers the question of when to reorder, the solution being to calculate the stock level that will take into account:

(i) the quantity of stock expected to be consumed in the period under review:

(ii) the lead time;

(iii) the amount of stock expected to be consumed during the lead time;

(iv) the establishment of a buffer stock to allow for contingencies such as an unexpected rise in consumption or exceptional delays in receiving supplies. Should the buffer stock be used, immediate action should be taken to expedite delivery as a stock-out is threatened.

Order quantity

It is a general business fact that the greater the amount of stock carried by a firm, the higher will be its stock holding costs. However, carrying a large stock will only necessitate the occasional stock holding costs, but to avoid a stock-out will necessitate making frequent purchase orders for each individual type of stock. This will result in high costs incurred by the purchasing department. There is clearly a conflict between stock holding costs which increase as more stock is held and purchasing costs which increase as less stock is held. Establishing a predetermined order quantity answers the question; how many should be ordered? The answer to this is the quantity that will reduce the total costs of purchasing and holding stock to a minimum. This is in fact the point at which holding costs equal purchasing costs, and is known as the economic order quantity. The economic order quantity can be established of each individual type of stock by using a mathematical formula or graphically.

Once the economic order quantity has been established for each material, it should be recorded and whenever the reorder level is reached a purchase order should be made out for that quantity. Reasons why the economic order quantity is important include:

(i) it should ensure total stock costs are minimized;

(ii) it enables maximum and minimum stock level parameters to be set, thus contributing towards the establishment of a good stock control system;

(iii) it facilitates automatic order procedure and is suitable for use in computerized stock control systems.

A stock control system will only be effective if forecasts of stock levels, rates of consumption, lead time and costs prove to be accurate.

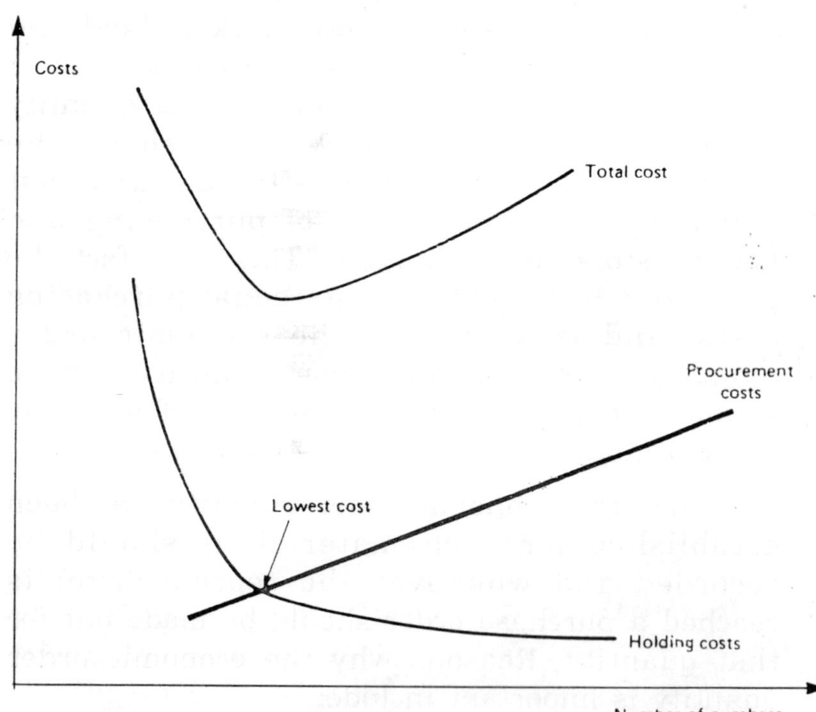

Outline example of a graphical method for determining an economic order quantity

Organization structure of the whole production function

An organisation chart portrays a typical organisation structure for the production function of a large manufacturing business. It should be studied carefully, the reader noting the relationship between many of the subdivisions discussed and where they appear. The following is important and should be remembered:

(a) The organizational structure of every business is likely to be unique. It should be designed to suit the individual needs of the business and will be influenced by:

(i) the size of the business;

(ii) the nature of the industry and products manufactured;

(iii) management policy;

(iv) the objectives of the business.

(b) The purpose of organising the production function is usually to produce an efficient, smooth-running and economical department that contributes to achieving the objectives of the organisation where they related to production.

(c) Ideally the production function should be represented at board level by a production director.

(d) The organisation structure should clearly show the responsibility of each department within the function in a way that will avoid confusion, ambiguity and conflict. Particular attention should be paid to this, as conflict and self-interest are most likely to occur where there is an overlap of responsibility between departments, e.g. quality control and purchasing are both responsible in some way for the quality of materials.

(e) Materials management has been included, but may, as an alternative, constitute a completely separate function responsible to senior management and not to the production manager or director.

(f) The production function is only part of the whole business organisation and must co-operate closely with and be co-ordinated with all the other functions.

3 Procurement Policy

Manufacturing organisations typically spend over half of their total sales revenue on the purchase of materials, components and services from outside organisations. Retailing organisations of course spend an even higher proportion, since what they sell is what they buy. In the case of manufacturing organisations, what they sell is what they make, and most of their purchases constitute the materials and components required for the manufacture of their products.

Although this chapter is mainly about procurement policy for manufacturers, a brief comparison between the situation for manufacturers and that for retailers will be useful to establish the policy variables. Any trading organisation needs to determine, and continually to reconsider, its market offering: what products it offers, what prices it charges, how its products are publicised or promoted and how they are distributed to the customer or to places-convenient to the customer.

A small independent retailer selects the products offered from those available at the wholesalers, cash and carry outlets, etc. A large chain store on the other hand may develop its own products and seek suitable producers for them. It may also purchase 'own brand' goods which are sometimes nationally available products, bought at a cheaper price without the national brand label. The main trading advantage of the chain store is in fact its ability to buy in bulk and thus both to rationalise its purchases and to get cheaper prices.

A small manufacturing firm will also make much use of wholesalers, and other organisations which specialise in supplying goods and services to manufacturers; but such organisations sell standard products, and even the smaller manufacturer needs to buy special products made to its own design. A large manufacturer may devote the major part of its purchasing effort to finding and trading with suppliers of components and materials which are not nationally available but are specifically called for by the design of the products which it is offering.

Very large manufacturers, and those occupying a de facto monopoly position as buyers, are in a position to exert so much leverage on their supply markets that they need to consider, whenever they take a major purchasing decision, the future state of the supply market which will result from it. Such organisations as the National Coal Board, British Telecom, IBM and General Motors constantly need to bear in mind such considerations, and much research and thought may be needed to decide whether a two-supplier market would be better than a three-supplier market, for instance.

The normal purchasing situation for the larger customer is what economists call bilateral oligopoly, that is, a small number of powerful suppliers dominate the supply market and a small number of powerful customers dominate the sales' market and a small number of powerful customers dominate the sales market. No formula will determine whether supplier or customer has the whip hand. Negotiation is used to decide the arrangements for supply: the specification, the contract quantity and the delivery quantities, the price and terms of payment, the inspection or quality assurance agreement, etc.

Procurement Strategies

Corey classified procurement strategies into three groups:

1. Cost-based negotiation
2. Market-Price-based negotiation
3 Competitive bidding.

While these were distinguished from each other basically by pricing mode, they also differed according to Corey in the product scope of the procurement (which could be narrow or broad), in the number and kind of suppliers contacted (ranging from one or very few in the case of cost-based negotiation to many in the second group), in price-quantity determination (including risk-sharing arrangements and the from in which quotations were requested) and in negotiating strategy (which varies considerably between the three groups).

Supplier selection was not just a matter of selecting the type and number of source, it involved the construction of a sourcing system in which different suppliers had different roles, for instance, technical development, price leadership, etc. Long-term supply availability, domestic versus foreign sources, distributors versus manufacturers and the strategy of numbers were some of the factors to be considered. Single sourcing and the stability of vendor relationships were topics of considerable importance, while in certain circumstances it could be quite difficult to persuade a supplier to accept an order. if a manufacturer needs to engage in demarketing its product, the customer needs to engage in marketing its demand, a reversal of the traditional relationship which may become increasingly prominent as material shortages loom larger.

Negotiation has become the subject of an enormous literature and many training courses are available for buyers, sellers, labour union representatives, management representatives, and many others with special interests. Most of this training material stresses the importance of the groundwork which precedes negotiating sessions, in which objectives are set, the relevant facts are assembled and conclusions drawn, and tentative agenda established for the negotiations.

Corey's work is based on research carried out at six very large American corporations during the seventies. Purchasing could be carried out, and in fact in all six cases was carried out, at plant level, divisional level, and corporate level; but a strong trend was noticed to centralise procurement decision-making to corporate level, mainly perhaps because of the increasing importance of the function as perceived by corporate management. Supply shortages and long-term planning of material availability, effective response to a changing business environment, profit improvement by mean of purchase cost reduction, and better selection, use and development of purchasing talent were listed as reasons for this trend.

Input management

Similar trends have been reported by Farmer in his discussion of the management of input to the firm form-its supply market. Input in the sense in which it is used here refers to the components and materials used in producing the firm's end products. It is argued that too many firms have confined their strategic planning to output management and the marketing of their end products, regarding the input area as operational rather than strategic. This thinking may indeed have been appropriate to the supply market conditions of the recent past, but it is doubtful if it continues to be appropriate in the present and likely that it will become quite inappropriate to future supply market conditions.

Farmer argues that while input management is one of the variables in a business system, and its importance varies from company to company and from time to time, it is nevertheless hardly ever to be regarded as insignificant. And while the operational aspects of input management are certainly important to the functioning of the business, it has strategic, aspects which have often been overlooked in the quest for operational efficiency of the various functions which are elements within it. Co-ordination and balance should be sought between the various functions, and between input and output management at the strategic as well as at the operational levels. to focus solely on cost reduction in the input and conversion stages of a manufacturing system, and to look for profit opportunities solely at the output end, may well, according to Farmer, have been major contributing factor in the decline and even demise of many manufacturing businesses.

Purchasing policy should thus be seen as part of business policy, purchasing strategy as part of business strategy. Long-term as well as short-term aspects need to be considered, as indeed they have been by successful Japanese manufacturers of motor cars, motor bikes, and TV sets, and by successful retailers such as Marks & Spencer.

Professor Farmer in this paper was looking particularly at the long-term and strategic aspects of supply planning; but the short-term and operational aspects are also important in the determination of procurement policy. Materials management planning, greatly facilitated by the more powerful computers and requirement planning, greatly facilitated by the more powerful computers and better systems which became available in the early 1980s, bought major improvements to supply and production operations in those companies which implemented it successfully. the insistence that management should devise and authorise a rational, feasible and appropriate master schedule, coupled with the ability to explode this into detailed schedules of what parts, components and materials to make or buy, week by week, over the whole planning horizon, came like a revelation to companies which had previously operated on a chaotic mixture of stock-controlled production and customer priorities.

Materials management was a different but related approach, also intended to improve operational efficiency, but his time by a change in departmental structures.

Materials management

The term 'materials management' presumably referred originally to the management of the activities within an organisation which had to do with the planning, purchasing, transport, storage and handling of the materials required by the organisation, using materials in the general sense to refer to the whole range of goods and service4s obtained from outside the organisation in order to provide finished products for sale. However, increasingly materials management has come to refer to the grouping together of these materials-related activities into one department under a materials manager.

In practice, surveys, have shown that adoption of some kind of materials management structure has been extremely widespread in the USA. and there has also been considerable interest in the UK; but the kind of organisation adopted has often not conformed to the theoretical approach shown in the diagram. It has been suggested that in seeking the organisation structure which is right for a particular company at a particular time, some key variables should be identified-such as:

1. Purchasing cost reduction leverage
2. Type of production make for stock or make to customer order
3 Commonalty of requirement between different divisions
4 Whether most problems occur between materials-related departments
5 Trade-offs between materials and non-materials departments.

These approaches are discussed more fully in Baily and Farmer, which also quotes evidence to suggest that the adoption of efficient computer systems for materials management appears to have reduced the need to combine the materials-related departments into a single materials management department.

It is obviously not easy to discuss the

organisational questions in the abstract because of the great variations in size, complexity and other dimensions which exist between companies. Several large concerns which operator a number of establishments favour some version of the materials management structure at plant level, where purchasing staff are grouped departmentally with stock control, stores, production planning and control, and transport staffs, while at corporate level purchasing and contracts staff from a separate planning and negotiating group. Similar developments can be seen in some retailing chains, where ordering and progressing staff are grouped organisationally with stock control, warehousing and transport, while a separate headquarters purchasing unit deals with the merchandising aspects, such as adoption of new lines and negotiation of original prices for first-time buys.

Devising appropriate organisation structures is a difficult process because so affected. Purchasing staff who have the ability to contribute to long-term strategy are not necessarily the same people as those who do a sound job of ordering and progressing regular requirements from established suppliers. Another factor arises from the fact that purchasing departments exist to arrange for the supply of goods in accordance with the requirements of other department, so that inter-departmental co-operation and communication is particularly important. Indeed many problems occur in practice in this area of inter-departmental relationship. An example is the matter of quality assurance, which forms the final topic in this chapter.

Purchasing and quality assurance

Of fundamental importance in purchasing is to make sure that the right quality of goods, materials, etc. is bought. Both technical and commercial considerations are involved. The purchasing department operates jointly with other departments which also have important roles to play in this crucial aspect of arranging for the supply be outside organisations of what is required.

Although a number of different activities or stages occur in the process of purchasing quality assurance, it is convenient to group them under two headings:

1. Specification quality
2. Conformance quality.

The first part of the process is concerned with specifying the quality required. This may consist of a comparison of available merchandise and the selection of suitable brands or standards, or it may involve the preparation of engineering drawings and other forms of internally prepared specifications. Such a specification is a detailed statement of the features or characteristics required in a material, part or product. These features or characteristics may include chemical composition, such physical characteristics as ductility, viscosity, conductivity, weight, colour, surface finish, and physical size or dimensions-to name a few. The tolerance should also be stated: that is, the range of values within which a characteristic may vary without making the product unacceptable

The Second part of the process is concerned with arrangements to ensure that goods received conform with the specification, and that their important features or characteristics are within the allowed tolerances.

Normally in manufacturing industries a specialist department such as design, engineering, standards, etc. is entrusted with the responsibility for specifications. Such a department needs to take account of inputs from marketing (what can be sold) and from purchasing (what can be bought), as well as the production implications. It is difficult to generalise about the role of the purchasing department in this connection beyond saying that it must play some part, and that its concern will naturally be with the commercial rather than with the technical aspects of the product. Commercial aspects include the relative cost and availability of alternative materials or products, and also the feasibility of obtaining the quantity required for bulk production at an acceptable price.

A single instance may illustrate the last point. A certain company manufactures agricultural chemical products, for use mainly by farmers but also by home gardeners. New products are continually being developed by the research and development laboratories. if approved by the new products committee, which is heavily marketing orientated, they are put into a two-year field trial process intended to uncover any unwanted side-effects as well as to provide evidence that the products will in fact produce the effect claimed. During this two-year period, a purchasing research section within the purchasing department investigates the availability on world markets of all the ingredients required by the formulation of each new product under trial. Naturally at the end of the two-year trial it is not possible to change the formulation before going into bulk production. But it would be a mistake for management to authorise bulk production if some of the ingredients could not be supplied in sufficient quantities.

The second part of the process is concerned with the selection of suppliers, the approval of their quality control systems and the inspection of goods received. Inspection is an expensive process, and should not need to be carried out at all if suppliers could be relied on to supply acceptable goods. Increasingly, purchasing organisations are taking steps to ensure that this is so.

Many organisations carry out their own investigations of suppliers, but third-party investigations are also used quite widely: the British Standards Institution, the Crown Agents and a number of other organisations operate in this connection. Most systems for investigating the quality capability of suppliers classify the work into three levels, depending on the extent to which the customer relies on the supplier.

At the simplest level, all that the customer needs to know is whether the supplier has satisfactory instruments, test equipment and inspection procedures for final inspection of his products.

Many intermediate-level products require inspection at a number of successive stages of manufacture, with a reliable system for corrective action if faults occur, so that a more comprehensive system of quality control would need to be certified.

When a supplier is responsible for design as well as for manufacture, the investigation of his quality capability needs to be still more extensive and thorough.

Industries such as aerospace, motor car manufacture, atomic energy and other parts of electrical manufacturing, are already subject to strict official regulation of certain aspects of quality (mainly those which have to do with safety) and this has been one of the factors leading to the development of British Standards such as BS 5179.

At the same time as official regulation of safety and other quality standards has increased, and official guidance as to procedures for ensuring that suppliers are capable of supplying and do in fact supply goods to the standard specified has become more widespread, a parallel development has been occurring within companies. Quality is everybody's business; job security and progression for the individual depends on the organisation's ability to survive and prosper, which in turn to a large extent depends on the quality of its products.

Quality circles are a recent example of many approaches which organisations have adopted to encourage individual and small group initiative in maintaining and improving the quality of the product.

Technical inspection of incoming goods is a costly business which in principle could be dispensed with if suppliers could be relied on to supply acceptable goods. The investigation and selection process described above is intended to ensure that suppliers are in fact to be relied on, nd is often used in practice to classify suppliers into three groups.

1. Accept goods on supplier's certificate
2. Accept goods after sample inspection
3. Impact all goods received; do not order from this supplier if an alternative supplier is available.

If goods received require technical inspection before acceptance, it is often possible to obtain satisfactory results by inspecting a sample rather than every piece submitted. A large body of theory exists which can be applied in this connection to select the size of the sample and to draw conclusions from the results.

4 Purchasing Procedures

Management will naturally wish to adopt or devise purchasing procedures which suit the individual requirements of their own organisations. Retailers do not in general use quite the same systems and procedures as manufacturers, while civil engineering contractors have their own variations: procedures need to be appropriate to the type of operation.

Some of the organisations which employ purchasing staff are quite small, while others are very large and operate on a national or a worldwide scale. Procedures can be affected by the scale of operation.

Procedures are also affected by the type of office technology employed. Communications between buyer and seller can be face to face, by word of mouth, handwritten or typed and sent through the post, or some form of electronic mail can be used. Telex and facsimile have been in use for many years. Communicating word processors, teletext and direct links between customer's computer and supplier's computer are in the early stages of adoption.

The standard operating procedure for purchasing will be affected by the type and scale of operation and by the type of communications and records employed, but in addition to the standard procedure, a number of special procedures may be used. For instance many organisations adopt special procedures for routine low-value purchases, and also for non-routine high-value capital expenditure transactions. Procedures need to be appropriate to the type of purchase, and to enforce a single standard procedure for all purchases, while having the merit of simplicity, is not always the best way to do things.

This chapter outlines a standard purchasing procedure in four successive stages:

1. Initiation
2. Supplier selection
3. Contract stage
4. Completion.

Reference is made in each stage to the special or non-standard variations most commonly encountered, with examples of forms.

Initiation

Purchasing for organisations involves arranging for the supply on time and at a suitable price of the goods and materials, equipment and merchandise, services and supplies which are required to meet production programmes, sales plans or operating needs. It is normally the job of the purchase department to make the purchase on behalf of production, sales or operating departments. it is not normally the job of the purchase department to determine what needs to be purchased: most purchases are initiated by requisitions from other departments.

A purchase requisition is a request to the purchase department from any other department for something to be purchased. It serves to initiate the purchase, and also for audit purposes to provide evidence of authorisation and action taken.

Such requisitions are date-stamped on receipt by the purchasing section and allocated to an appropriate member of department for action. The buyer may need to check the requisition against specification files, buying records and contract files. Some editing may be required, since requisitioners do not always express their requirements in terms suitable for communications with suppliers. if the item requisitioned is filed for a limited period in case of query: two years should be quite adequate.

Many stock items and MRO (maintenance, repair and operating) requirements are ordered several times a year, and for these a travelling requisition will save time. This is a card kept in the initiating department on which is entered permanent data (such as description) and variable data (such as quantity required and date). It is sent to the purchasing section to initiate a purchase. After ordering the goods, details are entered on the card which is returned to the initiating department.

Systems for production planning and control used by manufacturers, or for stock planning and control used both by manufacturers and service industries such as retailing, normally generate a large group of purchase requirements periodically. Rather than prepare separate individual requisitions for each item affected, a blanket requisition or schedule of requirements is produced.

Materials Requirement Planning (MRP) systems are particularly suitable for jobbing and batch production. With suitable adaptations they have been used in mass production ever since Henry Ford devised the first assembly line for motor cars. The process starts with the regular production or revision of a master production schedule which states, period by period, what quantities of each end product need to be completed to meet sales commitment or management plans.

For each end product the quantities due in each period are exploded by means of a parts list or bill of materials to determine what parts or materials are required for its completion, an this is offset by lead times to yield a time phased schedule of gross requirements for parts and materials. Adjustments are then made for uncommitted stock on hand and orders due in to produce a time-phased schedule of net purchase requirements, or blanket requisition.

Stock control systems fall into two main groupings:continuous, and periodic. In continuous systems, each stock item is assigned an order point and an order quantity. Whenever a stock item quantity falls to the order point, an order is triggered for the appropriate order quantity, so that the system produces orders continuously. Travelling requisitions as previously described are often used. In periodic systems, either the whole stock range or a substantial subsection of its is reviewed at regular intervals. Stock on hand is compared with target stock as previously determined, or as calculated dynamically from previously determined rules. A blanket requisition or schedule of stock replenishment requirements is produced.

Supplier selection

Upon receipt of a requisition, the purchasing section checks if the item in question is already covered by a contract. if it is, an order can be place against the contract without delay. If it is not covered by a contract, the next stage is to select a supplier and agree price and terms.

There is a strong preference for continuing to deal with regular suppliers in the case of regular purchases, so long as they continue to prove satisfactory. nevertheless it is advisable periodically to check the market, to see what other suppliers have to offer. How often this should be done is a matter for judgment, and will vary with the type and volume of requirement and the structure of the supply market. If the market is dominated by one or two major suppliers it may be greatly to the long-term advantage of purchasers to place their business in such a way as to keep competition alive. Very large purchasers which dominate a market on the customer side often devote a good deal of time and thought to the optimum supply market structure, and sometimes take direct action to support minority suppliers or to develop new suppliers.

It is good practice for purchasing staff to know their regular suppliers well, to be personally acquainted with the people who process and make decisions about their orders, to keep in touch with business plans, product developments and so forth. Suppliers are a major resource without which neither manufacturers nor traders could operate, and the management of supply markets can be a very important matter which calls for advance planning, forethought, and some difficult decisions.

When making a new purchase for which there is no regular supplier, or when checking the market for regular purchases, the usual procedure is to send a request for quotation to a short list of possible sources. Names of potential suppliers are obtained from trade knowledge of the buyers and their colleagues, advertisements and editorial material in the trade press, salesmen and technical representatives who call on the purchaser, and catalogues and other direct mail material which is received. A number of computerised buyers' guides are also available, which can be consulted on-line or by a telephone call, their main advantage is that they can be kept up to date continually, whereas printed directories can only be updated periodically when they are reprinted. As industrialisation spreads to new parts of the world, the search area for potential suppliers continues to widen; particular care should be taken before committing searching arrangements for important requirements to an entire divorces source, but major competitive advantage may result.

The form itself is simply the usual letterhead with, to savc typing, a standard preprinted text asking the addressee to quote price terms and delivery date for supply of the undermentioned goods on the terms and conditions stated overleaf.

There is, however, sometimes considerable scope to structure the request for quotation in such a way as to facilitate subsequent negotiation in order to arrive at a mutually satisfactory agreement which gives better value: alternatives may be put forward as total contract quantity sub-quantities to be ordered against contract or delivered in particular places at particular times, terms of payment and other aspect of the deal. In some cases suppliers are asked to support their price quotation by a cost breakdown, which will be compared with a price/cost analysis prepared internally by estimating staff attached to purchasing. This latter technique is particularly favoured by mass-production manufacturers, the very scale of which requirements limits possible suppliers to one or two in a given national cconomy.

In most cases the information a supplier gives on his tender or quotation needs to be supplemented by information in financial stability, quality capability, performance record, etc. which has to be obtained independently by purchasing staff. Reference was more in the previous chapter to supplier inspection visits in connection with quantity assurance. All these matters are of particular importance in sourcing new requirements or considering new suppliers. When considering regular purchases or established suppliers, the track record is of particular importance although it should not be forgotten change, new developments occur, new conducts are launched, new customers found; nevertheless it would not be prudent to ignore the record of how a particular supplier has behaved in the plan. Vendor rating is an attempt to systematise this information.

Vendor rating

Vendor rating, or supplier evaluation as its is come times called, is the process of systematically accumulating information about a supplier's actual performance and presenting it in numerical form. The usual aspects of performance to be measured are:

1. Quality.
2. On-time delivery
3. Service (although this is usually estimated rather than measured)
4. Price.

Quality is delivered or conformance quality: essentially, the proportion of goods delivered by a supplier which are accepted. In practice several rules are used to calculate a figure appropriate to the needs of a particular purchaser: one for instance is:

60 Number of batches accepted/number of batches delivered + 40 Number of parts accepted/ number of parts delivered

The delivery measure is again based on goods-received records and is essentially the proportion of goods delivered on time. Since the meaning of on time may not be the same in a large-scale mass producer and a small-scale batch producer, rules are specified to suit purchasing needs.

The price rating may be based on a comparison of the price quoted by the supplier in question with that quoted by competitors: the lowest price would score 100, and a price twice as high as the lowest would score 50 in one scheme. Often such a comparison is not feasible, and the price rating is based on a comparison of latest price with standard budget price, or last year's price, or latest target price.

It is not particularly difficult to calculate these ratings manually, since the system will be applied only to a minority of purchases from a relatively small number of suppliers, but computer salesmen have made much of the system as a further argument for extending the application of computers.

In most systems, after calculating individual numerical scores for the supplier characteristics being measured, a further calculation is made by weighting and combining the individual scores to arrive at an overall figure which is regarded as an index of the supplier's total performance - in fact a vendor rating or supplier evaluation figure which can be used in deciding how to allocate business between potential suppliers and also in persuading delinquent supplier to improve their performance!

Such systems are considered in more detail in purchasing textbooks, and in books about industrial marketing, but it must be admitted that recent accounts in books which have a practical rather than a strictly academic bias are somewhat less than enthusiastic about their use in practice and tend to stress their limitations. See for instance Baily and Baily and Farmer

The contract stage

A contract is business agreement for the supply of goods or the performance of work in return for a price, and subject usually to a number of terms and conditions. An order on the other hand is an instruction to a trader or manufacture to supply something.

In most cases both order and contract are incorporated in a single document, the purchase order from. Normal practice is to make it a rule that all purchases, subject to certain clearly defined exceptions, must be made by means of the official purchase order from. This if for practical rather than for legal reasons. The purpose of the rule is to prevent sharp practice. Whether by some unscrupulous employee or by some shady dealer outside the organisation, and also to establish clearly what the organisation is committed to accept and pay for. Regular suppliers are made aware of the rule by printing it on the order form, or by stipulating that the order number must be quoted on advice notes and invoices. Goods-receiving personnel can then be given instructions not to accept goods which are delivered without an official order number.

Exceptions to this procedure take several forms. The contract, or agreement with the supplier, may cover the supply of aggregated requirements over a considerable period of time, or over a large geographical area as when corporate contracts are signed by headquarters staff for common requirements at a number of divisions or branches. if such a contract is placed on the standard purchase order form it might course some confusion if the same form is also used for instructions to supply specific quantities of goods against the contract to specific locations.

Three solutions have been observed in practice. First, a special form is used for the contract document, and normal purchase order are used to order goods against it. Second, the normal purchase order form is used for the contract, and special forms are used for the orders; these may be known as delivery schedules, delivery instructions, contract releases, or call-offs. Third the same form is used both for order and contract, and care is taken to state on one: This is an order against contract and on the other, This is a contract against which goods should not be delivered until orders are placed.

Most organisations use a preprinted multipart set of forms for purchase orders. Four or five copies are usually provided, and these are distributed to supplier, goods receiving, possibly accounts, possibly originator, to purchase order open file, and possibly to order progress file.

Some large organisations have adopted computer-output order forms, which in the recent past appear to have largely failed to live up to expectations. The clerical work was not reduced, the amount of paper was increased because each order was confined to one item from one supplier, the technology was costly, and so on. But it is likely that such developments as communicating word processors, computer-to-computer links either via telex or telephone connection or several other methods currently being developed, will alter the balance of economics and that the traditional method of typed order forms sent by letter post will gradually become less economic than the newer methods of electronic mail.

Blanket orders or systems contracting methods are often used with considerable commercial advantage where it is possible to group together either numbers of different item requirements from one source, or else a sequence of requirements of one item over a substantial period of time, say, six months or a year. Instead of treating each order, or requisition, as an independent closed transaction, the idea is to look at the flow of requirements over a time and buy the flow, Instead of taking a bucket to the well every day, a waterpipe is laid on.

For example, a small or inter mediate value purchase in carbon paper. Instead of placing a series of order every months or so for the various size and grades required, with this technique once a year there is a review of requirements, alternative specifications and sources. Twelve months, requirements are then covered with just one or two orders which specify so many reams of A-4 standard weight, so many reams of lightweight, etc., to be delivered each month. If stocks start to build up or fall short during the year, one or two adjustments may be required. Apart from that, supplies come through automatically; and the price, based on a twelve-months contract, is low.

A group one or two production purchase may not seem at first glance amenable to this approach if production programmes are not fixed twelve months in advance. There will usually be a sales forecast going at least a year ahead, and a firm production programme going only one or two months ahead.

The solution then may be to approach management to authorise purchasing to make firm commitments for 50 percent of the sales estimate for the year, thus getting the benefit of a lower price and also the benefit of a bank stock of finished parts to handle cyclical fluctuations. In one actual case, component X was being bought in lots of 1000 approximately at a price of 26p a piece. It was built into a product with a current sales estimate of 12 000 a year. Contracting for 50 per cent of this, that is 6000 pieces, with delivery called off at 1000 a month, enabled the buyers to bring the price down to 20p, a 23 per cent reduction in invoice cost, with further reductions in administrative costs and paperwork. Both cost and availability are improved, and if sales fall short of forecast, it may well take nine or twelve months instead of six months to clear the components but they would still be used up within the year. This is a useful technique for plastic mouldings, castings, electrical and mechanical parts.

Small order procedures

Wherever possible the small orders should be put through a special procedure. If they are repeating or regular requirements they should be bought once a year in one lot, or perhaps twice a year: it is obviously uneconomic to expend 15 worth of man-hours, cheques, stamps and paperwork in procuring an item with a usage value of only 15 a year, but it happens. Non-repeating small orders are often such things as maintenance requirements, design and development prototypes, laboratory requirements. The requisitioner knows exactly what he wants and where to get it and the price is often a listed price. One solution to this problem is the order/ requisition/cheque form devised by Kaiser Aluminium in the United

States, and adopted by other organisations, including one in the public service. Through clever forms design, the same document which the requisitioner prepares as a requisition serves as an order, and a blank cheque accompanying it cuts out the invoicing/purchase-ledger/payments procedure.

Other approaches to the small order problem include: local cash purchase-a man with a bag of cash goes round in a van picking up requirements and paying for them as he goes; and laundry list-the local stockholder calls once a week and delivers a wide range of sundry materials against a laundry list type of order: invoices come through once a month and prices are negotiated annually.

The completion stage

Contracts (or orders) are completed when goods are delivered or work is done in accordance with the agreement and payment is made as provided.

Obtaining delivery on time can be a difficult problem: the sub-contract and component supply section of the engineering industries have got themselves a bad name for late delivery, although large numbers of purchasers throughout industry and commerce have few problems in this connection and would rightly regard late delivery as an exceptional event, to be dealt with by crisis measures when it occurs.

The fundamental step in obtaining delivery on time is to decide accurately and firmly exactly what is wanted at what time, to communicate this decision to those concerned, and to insist that delivery is made at the time specified. All too often firms which complain of late deliveries by suppliers are themselves to blame for inaccurate delivery schedules, continually amended. When both customer and supplier are struggling to operate with production planning and control systems which are defective in practice and misconceived in principle it is astonishing that anything is ever delivered on time, yet this has been the situation in certain sections of the engineering industry. Materials-requirement planning systems, if property designed and operated, have brought great improvements in this connection to manufactures of complex products.

The next step is to ensure that suppliers know that on-time delivery is a very important element in their marketing mix: in the combination of characteristics which results in their customers doing business with them. If valid due dates are stipulated it becomes easy to measure supplier performance in meeting due dates, and delivery performance tends to improve significantly once it is measured and reported. Customers with accurate, stable and reliable schedules of delivery requirements, who insist on delivery at the time scheduled, and measure and report supplier delivery performance, are on the whole quite satisfied with the results they get. In many cases it has been shown that 99 percent on-time delivery is normal when suppliers know and are fully aware that the schedule is accurate and that every time they fail to meet the schedule they are going to have to explain it to their customers. Nevertheless, progressing (chasing, expediting or follow-up) of orders remains necessary in many cases. This may be done:

1 At the date when tool or jig designs are to be ready

2 When the items from these designs should be available

3 When materials or components should be marshalled for production

4 When the various stages of production can be achieved

5. When final assembly and testing will be completed.

Often critical areas may be isolated in this progressing for special attention. For example, special castings with long delivery times could be delivered to suppliers and then be rejected because of their porosity. In consequence, some companies extend their progressing activities in such cases to include secondary suppliers.

Methods which can be applied to help ensure that more general orders are controlled - chased when they ought to be—include:

1 Copy orders filed in date-due order, being actioned, say, one week before that due date in general, or as necessary in the particular case.

2 Five divisions made at the top of the copy order numbered one to five. A signal of a different colour is then allocated to each month and one is attached to the relevant square in the particular case. The order copies are then filed in alphabetical order by supplier.

3 A diary system with the serial numbers of orders which are due being entered on the appropriate page of the diary.

Finally, the supplier dispatches the goods to the customer, usually including a packing note and copy advice note with the goods and also forwarding an advice note by post. The postal copy is passed to the purchasing section to note that goods are in transit and the same morning is passed on to the goods-receiving section. Each day the goods-receiving section check through their file of advice notes and if any goods appear to have been lost or delayed in transit they initiate appropriate action. When goods are actually delivered, a goods-received note is prepared, usually on a multipart form to notify purchasing, accounting, and originating sections of the delivery.

5 Purchase Accounting

The financial year

Drawing up estimates and a budget is only the beginning of a process which goes on throughout the year. The financial year does not always coincide with the tax year- it may be January to December, or the academic year. However it is organized, you can expect to receive information of expenditure from your accounts department at least once a month.

A monthly statement should include 'year to date' figures, i.e. those showing how much you have spent so far this financial year. You should also receive 'current transaction', i.e. figures for credits and debits made since the last statement. The figures should be allocated to the various cost codes you have available for credit and debit. A final figure will indicate how much money you have left to the end of the financial year. Computer printouts seldom print in red. You will have to look for any codes that imply you have a minus sum left for the year.

If you submitted detailed estimates, these

may also be shown alongside expenditure figures, thus giving a idea of how accurate your estimates were and whether any funds or 'heads' should be delayed for a while, or stepped up.

Monthly statement	*End of month 8*		*Library* Estimates	
Library grant	£550446.00 cr	($ 99082)	£55046.00 cr	($ 99082)
Sales and services	£3537.18cr	($ 6042)	£5000.00 cr	($ 9000)
Total Income	£58583.19 cr	($ 105449)	£60046.00 cr	($ 108082)
Printing and stationery	£158.00	($18284)	£300.00	($ 540)
Equipment rental	£1589.57	($ 2860)	£1000.00	($ 1800)
Photocopying	£400.00	($ 720)	£500.00	($ 900)
Library books	£12139.00	($21850)	£20000.00,	($ 36000)
Library periodicals	£12797.22	($ 23034)	£25000.00,	($ 45000)
Binding	£1084.30	($ 1951)	£4000.00	($ 72000)
Non-book material	£397.53	($714)	£380.00	($684)
Information services	£6242.29	($ 11235)	£8866.00	($ 15958)
Total Expenditure	£34807.91	($62654)	£60046.00	($ 108082)

From the example, it can be seen that on the whole the budget is on target two thirds of the way through the financial year. Equipment rental and non-book material are overspent while binding is way below target. This is probably because the annual binding time has not yet occurred 'Charged for' services are also on target to create the estimated income, and possibly more.

It looks as if only half the periodicals have yet been renewed for next year.

This is an example of a fairly helpful statement. You are just as likely to receive a statement which is covered with indecipherable codes, known only to accountants. It is not sufficient to keep jogging along, not understanding statements. You must ask what they mean.

The figures do not show what outstanding commitments the library has, and you should keep an account of these. It is never possible for a library to end the financial year with all orders fulfilled. However, for the sake of the accounts department you will need to know what orders you have outstanding, and what payments are due to the library. Again, keeping separate records of these is important information for your managers and for you when you are trying to make a case for more money next year. Also, you may need to adjust your estimates during the year. Keep your managers informed of problems such as the relative strengths of various currencies, or cash flow problems as charged services are not paid for at once.

The amount of record-keeping you will need to do for individual orders and payments will vary depending on where you work. As a minimum you should keep one copy of each order sent out and one copy of each invoice paid. Auditors like accession registers and invoice ledgers. Busy Librarians do not. You can, explain that catalogues take over from accession registers and that copy invoices replace ledgers in which each bill is individually entered. In practice, your accountant will be producing a ledger every time they pay an invoice or receive credit.

You should note on invoice copies the data on which you send them to the accounts department for payment so as to help you check statements from suppliers. Statements ae sent out by suppliers at regular intervals. If your accounts department does not pay within the time stated on an invoice you will receive a statement showing invoices unpaid. Beware: statements are often printed on exactly the same stationary as invoices. Look for the word *statement*. Some accounts departments will check statements for you, but if neither of you does and bills are left unpaid, you will receive a beautifully embellished solicitor's letter. It is not worth risking these very often. If you do receive one, resolve the problem at once for your peace of mind and the library's internal competency rating.

Every so often your accounts will be thoroughly checked by an auditor. The most common auditing method in libraries is to use an audit trail. The auditor will follow an individual order through from raising the order to receipt and payment. They may well want so see the item itself as well as its paid invoice. They may also consider wider issues such as value-for-money if you have a publications exchange programme or the handling of a Value Added Tax on charged services.

It is up to the librarian to show the value of the library service, both in monetary and quality terms. You cannot do this unless you have a clearly worked out budget, careful cost accounting throughout the year, and both of these linked to the stated aims and objectives of the service. Accounting for staff time as a feature of your costs is part of a professionally prepared budget.

6 Purchase Budgeting

Background to the budget

Whether you are setting up a service from scratch or taking over the budget function, there are several points you must find out from your organisation before drawing up any financial estimates. You should talk to the manager who has responsibility for the library budget, and to the accountant(s) and those people who actually handle payments on behalf of the library. On the whole, accountants have scant understanding of the multiplicity of orders and invoices involved in the provision of information, and a personal link will help ease any problems you may have in the financial year ahead.

Some of the questions you will need answers to are:

- Who has overall managerial responsibility for the library budget?
- Who has day-to-day responsibility for the library budget?
- Who has authority to sign invoices for payment for the library?

- Who actually handles the library's accounts?
- When (in the month) are invoices paid?
- Are payments sent electronically/by cheque?
- How do you get a cheque raised quickly?
- How do you get petty cash quickly?
- Is there a central purchasing department? (If so, how does it affect you? Are you obliged to order everything via them?)
- It the library considered to be the central purchasing department for all printed material even if it is not intended for the library?
- What happens if you overspend/underspend?

With the answers to these questions, and any other information you may have already on library use (or non-use), you can begin to draw up a budget. Bear in mind what you already know about your organization in terms of which parts of it are flourishing and which are not doing so well. Try to align yourself with the first.

How much money will you get

Formula-funding represents perhaps the least complex form of funding, where the library receives a percentage of the income of the organisation it serves, or perhaps a percentage of its research budget. This is not a very helpful way of funding, since it cannot take into account the particular needs of information units, as opposed to other parts of the organization, which have different responsibilities.

Lump sum funding means exactly what it says; the library receives the amount of money that the organization believes it deserves. The library will need to break it down into meaningful segments.

Incremental funding takes into account various factors; what happened last year, inflation trends, currency trends, the way in which the business is heading, financial constraints, and growth plans.

Departmental accountants and corporate planners can be very helpful by explaining current constraints and opportunities. However, librarians should not get too excited about their ability to actually influence the amount of money they get. You can only make the best case possible on your behalf.

Drawing up a budget

Library budgets can range from the very simple budget to those which are broken down into a variety of different areas, heads, funds or account codes. Examples of different kinds of budget are given later in this chapter.

The method of budgeting used in other departments of your employing organisation will probably also be used in the library. This may be line-by-line, performance budgeting, or zero-based budgeting, but it is worth familiarizing yourself with various types as each has useful attributes.

Usually, the librarian or equivalent will draw up a draft budget or estimates that will initially be discussed with the line manager who collates budgets from various departments. After any necessary changes it will go to higher management for approval. The library manager may be called on to defend the budgetary figures at this stage, so you must know what you are talking about.

Always draw up a clear and simple budget. Accompanying explanatory notes should appear on separate pages. Draw it up in a professional-looking way so as to influence decision-makers. Senior managers have enough negative feelings about the competencies of librarians without you adding to them. Always have plans ready for all contingencies:

- What you could buy with more money
- What you could cancel if necessary
- What plans you have for the future
- What was right/wrong with last year's budget
- What comparative units are spending elsewhere

Remember that bad news well presented will go down better than good badly presented. Senior managers do not want surprises.

Line-by-line budgeting

Here is an example of a line-by-line budget for a commercial scientific research library:

1. Books and pamphlets £45 000 ($ 81 000)
2. Periodicals £100 000($18 000)

3.	Microform	£1000($ 1 800)
4.	Binding	£3000($ 5 400)
5.	External information	£97 000($174 600)
6.	Translations	£15 000($ 27 000)
7.	Inter-library loans	£15 000($ 27 000)
8.	Internal information	£25 000($ 45 400)
9.	Private (i.e. not library) books	£13 000($23 400)
	Total	£314 000($56 200)

Line-by-line budgeting is also known as incremental budgeting, as it is simply extrapolating next year's budget from what happens this year. It is relatively easy to understand and draw up, however, it can allow for too much inertia and mask a lack of serious thought about the library service. It leaves little room for new developments or for contingencies, although new lines or codes can be added. It does ensure that money is allocated to existing known needs.

The example given has no figures for staff or their associated costs such as travel or training, since this is handled separately. Equally, there are no figures for capital equipment, furniture or maintenance. Again, these are usually kept separate, and new items to be purchased involve making a special case.

An even simpler example of a budget from a management consultancy information unit follows:

1. Library cost debit £20 000 ($36 000)
2. Library costs credit £20 000 ($36 000)
3. Date costs debit £25 000 ($45 000)
4. Data costs credit £25 000 ($45 000)
5. Journals and books (net) £40 000 ($72 000)

Here, budget items mirror each other. The information unit charges out its services to the consultancy group, so as the library uses an information broker or an inter-library loan the cost is entered on line 1; when the charge made is recouped it is entered on line 2. Data costs for on-line searching are entered on line 3, while the recouped charges are entered on line 4. The money the unit may spend on books and journals is a net sum which cannot be billed out to clients. Actual estimates will show figures in 1 and 3 to be mirrored in 2 and 4, respectively. Charging for services is considered in more detail later in this chapter.

Performance budgeting

Budget examples given so far provide no evaluation of the service. They are concerned with input rather than output. Performance budgeting starts from a cost-benefit analysis of the service. Unit costs are developed for each activity, with emphasis being laid on effectiveness and accountability.

The first widely used type of performance budgeting was Planning Programming Budgeting Systems (PPBS). This provides an analytical approach to budgeting where the three elements of planning, programming and budgeting are integrated. For this system you have to develop clear objectives, identify outputs, measure these outputs, and analyse the benefits in relation to the cost: A general example could be:

Inputcost	**Category**	**objective**
£8 000 ($14 400)	Current awareness service	Promote awareness of library services
Output	**Cost per output**	
60 bulletins	£8 ($14.4)	

Zero-based budgeting

It is certainly no coincidence that zero-based budgeting came to prominenance in libraries at a time when they were being squeezed, by and with their parent institutions in the 1980s. This system involves justifying all expenditure from scratch, or from a zero base.

Decision packages are prepared by looking at specific activities and their purpose or goal, and the advantages of retaining the activity or the consequences of stopping it are considered. Then a cost table can be drawn up showing cuts in the activity, retaining the status quo, and increases in the activity. An example hypothetical decision package framework is:

Name of Activity:

Purpose of Activity:

Advantage of Retention:

Consequence of Elimination:

Alternatives

Budget	Description	Cost
80%		
100%		
120%		

With this sort of form, which can easily be set up on a microcomputer with a spreadsheet package, you might, for example, have to consider the telephone provision of information to remote branches of your organization. Why do you do this? Would it be a good idea to continue? What would happen if you stopped? Then you need to cost out a cut in this provision (80%), the retention of the status, quo (100%), and an increase in the service (120%). Of course, this presupposes that you already log all your calls and have worked out the cost of staff time involved. Nothing is ever as simple as it seems on a form.

ZBB is very time consuming, although it does have the advantage of making you look critically at the service. It is often forced on special libraries, particularly where managers have no idea what a library can provide, nor why this unknown provision seems to cost so much. Some employers take the system at face value and work up from a zero base: 'Imagine that the library budget is nil; how would you justify the purchase of x..? It is to be hoped that you won't have to do this every year.

It is best, if possible, to combine elements of several types of budgeting: line-by-line budgets show how money will be divided up: ZBB provides criteria to justify services and, with performance measures, shows how the service is operating in terms of its aims and objectives.

Purchasing and charging

Purchases

The main purchase for any library is information, which comes in many forms as materials (books, journals, data) and services (online, information brokers). You need staff to exploit this information as well as the space in which to operate and the necessary equipment. All these factors have to be considered as part of your budget.

Materials

Your usual material purchases are likely to be books, journals, conference proceedings, reports, and working papers, government publications, and trade/professional literature. It goes without saying that you should try to get the best value for money by obtaining discounts where possible but, on the whole, speed of supply and accuracy are likely to be ahead of price on your list of priorities.

Find suppliers who can handle your requirements and work out, for example, how to get the latest government report on the day it is published. This can mean you or your staff going personally, cash-in-hand or paying a courier.

Library users have little idea of the difficulties of purchasing or obtaining obscure reports. If you cannot buy what the user wants, try borrowing from another library. Build up a network of other libraries that will help, and offer help to them in return when it is needed.

Buying individual books and reports is usually a well accepted practice in special libraries, but ongoing orders for periodicals or expensive annual reference books can be harder to justify. Serials are also an ongoing commitment in staff time for check-in, chasing, binding and circulation. They are vulnerable to cuts. Some libraries 'charge out' periodicals or serials to individual departments which have a particular interest in the subject matter, but this means they no longer belong to the library and control over them is lost. Try to use prepayment discounts for these items from supplier such as the Sweets and Blackwell subscription services. They will also be able to offer advice on currency fluctuations

Selection of what materials to buy is in practice the librarian's task. Of course, you should react to suggestions from your library users, but you must keep up with what is going on in your organization as a whole. Try to purchase ahead of need. For instance my library committee rejected the purchase of expensive statistics on China, but once they arrived one member of the committee used them all the time for a new project. Use bookseller alerting services such as the slips from Bumpus, Haldane and Maxwell.

Buy specialist items from the specialist suppliers, e.g. Collets specialized in material from Eastern Europe.

Beware of donations to the library. There is no such thing as a free book, despite the well known belief of library users BLOTSBYTS. Donations are a cost to your service.

Of course, the collection you build up is unlikely to consist only of bools and journals You will have to consider such formates as software packages, trade literature and indexes, video, slides, and CD-ROM, as well as in-house databases.

Try to keep records of total materials spending, average costs per item, and how much is spent on each department of your organisation. This can be fed into your budget planning next time around together with publicly available price indices.

Services

The services most commonly purchased for special libraries are on-line search services, and information brokerage or information consultants. On-line services are confusing in their different methods of charging, further complicated by their willingness to negotiate terms related to access and volume of use. You may want to account for annual changes to a database host as a materials purchase and actual on-line costs as a services purchase. Of course, on-line services not only provide your clients with more information, but also push up the demand for further information provision, in particular inter-library loans.

Inter-library loan is crucial for small units in the provision of material outside your normal subject area or only needed occasionally, material which cannot be purchased or which is too expensive to purchase. Electronic transmission of requests and the use of available periodical and accession lists should speed up your service, Translations are a specialized are where you may have to purchase outside services.

If there is limited staff you will have to use information broker services to cope with 'I need it yesterday' requests. Extensive and expensive use of such services may help make the case for more staff in-house at a later date. Records of such costs mist certainly be kept.

You may also want to use consultants to help establish a new service, design or redesign the physical set-up of your service, overhaul your existing service, or indulge in systems analysis. On the whole, this is work you could do yourself if you had the time.

For bought-in service, the question then is do they:

- reduce costs?
- speed access to information?
- provide better quality information?

The way in which you order these considerations will depend on the priorities of the organization for which you work. Payment for an automated library system can also be considered as a purchased service.

Staff

The cost of staff is usually the largest part of your total budget. At least 50% and up to 80% of the budget can be used in this way. In the budget you will have to consider existing staff and any temporary or new staff you expect to recruit for special projects. Advertising and interview expenses can be substantial. The cost of training and staff development should also be planned, along with any increment or special payments due. Apart from actually paying staff, there are indirect costs such as National Insurance and pension payments which could add another 50% to the staff bill.

Your organization is likely to set salary ranges, hours, special payments and fringe benefits and, of course, holidays. While you may have little say in these beyond the level of recommendations to the personnel department, the advantage to you may be that staff are not considered as part of your annual budget. Nevertheless, you should still keep careful records of grading, job descriptions, incremental or long-service payments, and pension scheme membership.

Space

Some libraries and information units are charged by their organizations for the space which they occupy. These charges can include lease, or rent, mortgage, business rates, and heating and power. The advantage of this system is that a clear indication is given of what the library actually costs the institution in space terms. The library manager is unlikely to be able to change the system.

On occasions, these kinds of payments will be indirect, being absorbed by the parent organization, but you should not ignore their existence. You may still be charged maintenance charges even if you are not charged rent. Space charges are an overhead you will need to cover when accounting for your services

Equipment

The most obvious equipment purchases for libraries are office supplies, stationery, printing, furniture, etc. However, much more expensive items such as microcomputers, fax machines and photocopiers may also be considered as equipment. You may work for an organization that buys these for you, or arranges fixed or phased payback arrangements so that your budget is not hit too hard all at once. For large pieces of equipment, sometimes known as capital equipment, you may have to make a special case for funds. Plan this well ahead to avoid disappointment, and make sure to obtain good prices, and be seen to be doing so.

Much large equipment carries associated recurrent costs such as telephone bills, leasing arrangements for photocopiers, maintenance contracts for computers, and there may also be insurance. You may have to maintain a sinking fund to amortize the cost of equipment, and possibly plan for repurchase.

Library computer systems always have ongoing costs, and you must try to plan for these. They usually appear as an annual charge. If you are allocated money for equipment each year, always make sure to spend it. If you do not it will be assumed that you do not need that amount in another year.

Contingencies

Last, but by no means least, you will need to leave room in your budget for contingencies and irregular payments. Some examples are:

- Special payments to staff/overtime/overlapping appointments/entertainment
- Interest payments on purchases of capital equipment
- General book fund for immediate urgent purchases.

Although it is seldom possible to forecast what immediate needs may arise during the financial year, you should still assume that something unforeseen will arise. However, do not leave any money for contingencies in your budget at the end of the year. You should always be spent to the budget. This is easier said than done, particularly if you are earning money as well as spending, since you will also have to depend on the efficiency of the accounting procedures of your clients. If you have money left over, now is the time to consult your list of what you could purchase if you had the money.

Purchasing strategy: On-line versus paper

The purchase of access to on-line services is viewed as one method of collection management. If you cannot afford the money to buy printed materials, on-line services can give you access to them, this despite the recent assertion from an officer of the Publishers 'Association that a paperless library is about as likely as a paperless toilet!

The conflict between the purchase of print of on-line can be considered under various headings:

- Does on-line access mean that you can cancel printed subscriptions?
- Are you restricting the number of information users at a time, by only providing one computer terminal or intermediary as opposed to several printed volumes?
- How many of your customers already have their own on-line access and are therefore less likely to make use of the library service?
- Does on-line impose extra stress on your service by suggesting material you will have to obtain from elsewhere?
- Can your budget cope with increased costs of on-line services?
- Can you keep up with the proliferation of databases and their associated learning curves?
- Do you need to set up a new budget fund or code for on-line?

- Do you need to buy new equipment and furniture?
- Would it be more cost-effective to buy in outside expertise from an information broker or on-line search service?

As you can see, many of the considerations are budgetary, but there is no doubt that whatever kind of service you provide you must make provision in your budget for obtaining material promptly from elsewhere. Inter-library loans are the first obvious route, but you should also have links with other services similar to your own so you can exchange material or simply provide each other with specialist material rapidly. Cooperation breeds cooperation.

Charging for your service

The increasing cost of providing on-line search services has acted as a catalyst in the move towards charging customers for information. Although some would argue that it is a cost-effective means of collection management. This is not the place in which to discuss the pros and cons of charging, but it is important to consider *how* to charge.

Given the substantial historical basis of the free public library service it has taken time for libraries to move towards charging for services, and librarians are seldom trained in the necessary skills. If a special library is a cost centre it may appear to accountants as just one more department amongst many, an overhead of sorts where the library cannot generate its own funds and may not strictly be aware of its own status as an overhead. If, on the other hand, the library is a profit centre, the value of its services becomes more obvious in monetary terms, and it must take active responsibility for overheads or salaries, training, computer and printed information.

The simplest way to charge for information is to 'charge out' the acquisition of material to departments outside the library. For example, you may purchase a very expensive periodical that is only used by one department and you could charge the subscription to that department. Another method of charging out would be to charge the direct costs on-line searching. However, neither of these examples really tackles the actual cost of providing the service. For example, neither takes into account staffing costs.

Setting charges

Setting a charges for the provision of information must take into account the following factors:

- What is the realistic cost of staff? Assess available hours plus administration and development of service and training of staff. Staff are not 100% efficient all the time, and they do need holidays.
- What is the unit cost for provision of each type of information. Unit costs are not performance measures. Cost does not necessarily reflect value for money. On-line charges are complex, and you may need to fix a price for each piece of information.

How can you spread costs realistically? If you have high fixed costs, unit costs can decrease with volume of requests, e.g. the second time you answer the same question it will be much cheaper to provide the answer. If you have low fixed costs, the revenue earned can more easily match actual costs. Fixed costs are staff, accommodation etc.

- How can you set charges? The relationship of costs to 'sales' must not change dramatically over time, which means you should try to set an acceptable charge from the beginning. Dramatic changes in price or complicated pricing will upset customers. You must obviously price at a level your customers can afford, and be able to answer the question 'What do I get or my money?' Some idea of what prices are charged elsewhere would be useful.
- How should customers pay? Retrospective charging or estimation will lead to cash flow problems and invoicing bureaucracy. You may already have to pre-pay on-line service subscriptions. If you charge by subscription this will provide money up front, but your service will be scrutinized on renewal. Obviously, it is easy to charge a subscription for such items ad library bulletins. Charging involves a good deal of administrative work in invoicing, etc.
- Where will money come from for development of new services? Variable costs include volume

of sales, extra staff, and equipment and marketing. These will need to be budgeted for so that new developing services can 'piggyback' on existing services while they develop. This consideration can underline the tension between serving the institution and encouraging new uses and users of information. Your costs should therefore be related to the aims and objectives of your service.

7 Maintain Enough Stock

"We should have three months' stock on the shelf to meet customer demands," said one executive. Another stated, "The customer wants delivery tomorrow, and in our business he gets it."

Both men clearly understood where paychecks come from. Both were determined to ship promptly. But there could be big differences in the amounts of inventories carried by their two companies. The first might have two months' supply of pig and scrap iron in its foundry yard, take one month to process its product, and then carry three months' stock of finished articles. Total inventory is represented by six months' supply. The second may also have two months' stock of raw materials, say chemicals, but be able to turn out some compounds today and ship finished products tomorrow. In this case, the total inventory is, comparatively, only one-third as much, disregarding costs. The total time equivalent of raw and finished inventory is about one month, in a modern automobile-producing plant.

Three stocks

These examples suggest three types of stock that must be maintained. They are commonly called raw materials, work in process, and finished stock. Large companies may have more groups. For instance, work in process can be in transit-moving from a fabricating plant to an assembly center. Too, finished stock may be at plants, in transit, or spread all over the country in warehouses, on consignment, or in dealers' stores.

On the other hand, some companies have comparatively little finished stock. Two reasons occur to me. One is that the products are both too big and too expensive to keep. Locomotives, ships, heat exchangers, cracking units, and turbogenerators are examples. These also suggest the second reason, namely that the products are made to order. Both types are shipped as soon as finished. They are "cleared" from work in process to finished stock merely by paper transactions to keep the books in order.

The usual company, however, has all three kinds of inventory. It tries to carry enough raw materials to meet foreseeable demands. It has work in process as long as manufacturing continues. And it carries some finished stock if only such items as nuts, bolts, and washers bought on the outside.

Hobble Along

All three stocks represent money tied up. In reality, they are three stages of one stock. Therefore, while each will be discussed in turn, the comments made about any one are applicable generally to all three.

You know that the objective of control is to achieve an economical balance between the costs of ownership incurred to avoid customer disappointments on the one hand and on the other the costs of those disappointments. This is difficult to do.

For one thing, few managers have put dollar signs on the costs of customer ill-will. Of course, this varies over a wide range. At the low end may be a solicitous phone call or a martini lunch to smooth his ruffled feelings. At worst, you must get a new customer. Even this cost varies, considering the resistance of competitors to raiding and the extent of profit in whatever replacement sales can be made.

Without values, neither managers nor computers can answer the question, "How much inventory?" Consequently, many managers hobble along trying to hold down inventories and still meet demands. These are pictorial only. They show the balance managers try to achieve.

Inventory maintenance

Carrying costs rise as they attempt to improve customer service. These costs head skyward as perfection is approached.

Also, the amounts of carrying costs vary greatly. They are said to range from 15 to 30 per cent. The major items are interest or return on investment, damage or deterioration, and obsolescence. Obviously, these per cents differ markedly among types of products.

Costs like deterioration and obsolescence are offset by holding down inventory. So are carrying charges. But some of such gains are spent in more frequent reorderings. Thus, the two lower costs are somewhat interchangeable. And as one is traded for the other, the point of lowest total shifts.

Finally, there is the cost of profits lost. This may be either or both of sales lost or expenses contracted in pacifying customers. And they will differ with conditions. At one extreme might be low profit losses because customers can't get the product from any other source. Similarly, buyers may be trained to wait long periods for tailor-made items.

In contrast, the losses may be high because customers can buy from dozens of vendors vying with each other to get the business. And too, this phase of cost depends upon the potential profit in the sales that may be lost.

Three factors

Behind the overall picture just outlined are the volumes of inventory. These depend upon diversity to a large extent. Each different kind, size, or shape may require some amount of safety stock.

Too, of course, is the time length of the process cycle. This may have a relatively low cost n that much of the time is spent in waiting, heating, drying, or aging. Or costs may be high because the time cycle is lengthened by the many operations performed.

The time cycle is altered by a third factor-customer-service policy. Surely a policy like the opening comment "...in our business he gets . . delivery tomorrow" will end to increase finished stocks.

Correct material

Among all these complexities, managers usually have more leeway in the control of raw materials. They have process cycles as time cushions to work with. Yet they must face the other problem oı keeping the work force producing effectively. This phase should be well taken care of by sound scheduling. Unfortunately, though, pressure to keep the ship going will sometimes result in using raw materials that the available instead of those prescribed.

Such mistakes can be fourfold. First, waste is increased. Second, quality may be altered or ruined. Third, later jobs are robbed of material. Lastly, storage, damage, or congestion costs may go up because you can't ship the product.

Certainly, there are emergencies. These should be very few, however, when Production Control schedules work to be done only after making sure that materials will be on hand. In addition, the other functions of your organization must help to prevent intermediate errors.

1. Engineering must specify the kind and amount

of raw material to use. And when there is any choice, as with sheet metal, which way to cut it.

2. People in charge of stores must properly identify the material and locate it where it can be readily found.
3. Material handlers must have enough stick-to-itiveness to find the right material and deliver it to the correct location.
4. Supervisors or employees must check identification to see that the material delivered is the one specified.

You may not have the problems that can come out of material substitution. Yet, you can understand the best of planning can be upset by faulty material consumption.

Organize materials

In any event, event, experience suggests that Production Control should determine material requirements and see that they re ordered. In conjunction with this step, it is obligated to get delivery promises. These may be established in a routine way by notifying Purchasing of production needs according to lead times furnished and kept up to date by them.

Working with lead times is important. The opposite, getting materials in a hurry, is too expensive. So also is the common practice of purchasing for individual orders. Try to avoid the one-at-a-time habit I have seen so often. Why treat each order as though it were the only one in the plant? Your buyer should not be put in the position of ordering six 15/8-inch bolts in the morning and four 15/8-inch bolts that afternoon

You should organize the task of determining material needs if this task has not already been done. To this you may say, "That's Engineering's job." If it were, I'm convinced you'd have more standardization of materials.

Material card

In the meantime, your problems will be reduced, and so will the costs of getting materials, if you do the work. One way to start is by assigning code numbers to your raw materials. Any numbers will do. Still you're better off in the long pull, if you take time to devise an indicating arrangement of numbers. For instance, if you are in metal fabrication, you might say, "We'll use 1 for cold-rolled, 2 for stainless, and 3 for aluminum,"

Your second set of one or two digits might designate shape like sheet, round, rectangle, angle, or channel. You could assign a their pair of digits to signify sizes of raw stock. The purpose of the code is to collect in one place all items made from a specified material. Such a code number was shown as Material 114 on the Operation Sheet.

At the left of the card you see listed all part numbers made from Material 114. This is a very instructive record. It has many uses in any well-organized company.

Raw materials

For Production Control, you should create and maintain it as a link in material ordering. To make this work easier, you compute decimal equivalents that parts are of unit materials.

In the case of 48321, you need 231/2 inches for each piece. Dividing this length into the 16 feet of a unit bar gives an answer of 8.16 pieces per bar. If. 16 is enough allowance for cutoff, and all 16 feet of the bar are usable, then you can count on 8 parts per bar. Number 48321 then takes. 125 (1/8) part of 1 unit of material.

All this basic information is reproduced as often as you need it. For example let's think of monthly scheduling. Some way, and I'll discuss several in this book, you find you will need 420 of 48321 to meet your schedule. This quantity times the decimal equivalent comes out 53 units (bars). In the same way, you determine the raw material you will need for the other parts. The total of code 114 is 87 units for the period.

Scrap added

One more vital detail. What about scrap? You have at least three ways to add on. The best, if you are working with either large quantities or sizable per cents, is to record your adders on the material cards. I would put these in separate columns to the right of part size. In this form, you can adjust the per cents according to experiences. Their inclusions will increase decimal equivalents.

An easier but less exact way is to add some

average per cent to the total. If this is close enough for your operations, I would print the word "Scrap" above "Total" on the card. Alongside, your should note the per cent to be computed and added. These notation will serve as reminders to provide for shrinkage.

Minimum cushion

A third way is to rely on a cushion of stock to take up the slack. This is the method used by most of the managers who have progressed about half-way toward what I believe to be practical control.

Certainly, the system of routine reordering when minimums are reached entails much less work than the method I have recommended. Moreover, safety stock cushions can be kept small if your output is quite steady throughout the year.

Seasonal demands

In contrast, many companies must contend with seasonal low and high demands. Such variations can mean that you might carry too much stock in dull periods and yet run out during peak times. Observe also, that if you were to raise the minimum to prevent running out, you would greatly increase the amount of stock carried when you didn't need it.

This is the erroneous assumption that customers will buy the same amounts at the same times they did in prior periods. Of course, you must make some such guesses in order o gain the advantages of routine reordering. But you know that annual volume tends of move up or down from an average.

You can have all of interferences with lead times that may delay the arrivals and flows of materials. Keep in mind, then, the differences between theoretical systems and practical conditions.

To straddle the variations, you should alter the quantities ordered. Yet you can see that in theory, stock never ran out. Said the other way, you can operate with less inventory when you order materials as you need them if you are willing to run out to the same extent as with the routine min-max.stock control.

Level work load

Running out of stock creates problems and costs. These were hinted at earlier when I mentioned substitutions. Using acceptable material is ingenious. It avoids headlines in the evening paper reading PLANT SHUTS DOWN. The alternatives are paying for waiting time or sending some people home.

Having people and equipment wait may be cheaper. A plant in Passaic, New Jersey, has proven that turning out another product ahead of schedule is more costly. However, supervisors persist in assigning any work available. They make this wrong choice because of their training by topside managers to strive for volume of output.

At the least, you have an inventory shortage somewhere. Maybe the incoming material cannot be used as replacement. Eventually you may have to contend with another rush order, a delay in deliver, or higher costs caused by avoiding customer disappointment.

All this emphasis about providing materials is deliberate. Obviously, you can't start without them. But much that has been stressed applies also to purchased parts, work in process, and finished stock. Values are different, sure. However, the balancing of ownership cost against delivery timeliness is the same problem.

Purchased parts

For example, parts you but from a vendor must arrive on time if you are to ship your customer's order when promised. ANd, as I often say in one plant, "This includes labels for our boxes."

You may classify elements, parts, or assemblies as raw materials. Technically they are. Generally, however, their uses are more restricted. Many cannot be utilized for any other than the specific purposes for which they were bought. Also, you can't get many such items around the corner from a local warehouse. Further, you may get caught in a squeeze if these fabricated items fail to pass your incoming inspection.

So you start sooner. You induce Purchasing to find several reliable suppliers. You ask for reasonable lead times. You want these vendors to keep the inventory up to almost the last minute.

To gain this reduction in money tied, up, you may have to do two other things:

1. G[illegible] P[illegible]ing to work out some form of

blanket order. This is a way of telling your suppliers how many you will want in a period like six months or a year, with intermediate shipping dates and quantities.

2. Induce Quality Control to "qualify" the vendors so you have assurances that the items can be used when they arrive.

Economical lot

In ordering, consider economical lot size. Here again, you try to balance alternative costs. In buying, these are all the expenses created by procuring a lot. Against these are matched the expenses of owning it. The major comparative costs may be those in the following lists:

Getting	*Owning*
Production-control request	Interest
Purchase order	Deterioration
Purchase order	Deterioration
Receiving	Damage
Inspection	Obsolescence
Handling	Storage space
Storing	Insurance
Inventory record	Taxes
Accounts payable	
Invoice payment	
Waiting time	

In your business, some of these costs may not

exist. Instead, you may have others. In any event, the balancing of costs is the same problem we have always associated with manufacturing.

Manufacturing order

These quantities were developed for the job ship range of lot sizes. They apply whether you buy or make. The differences in the two conditions, as you know, lie in the types of costs included.

For example, setup cost for making an item in your plants would include the scrap that usually occurs in turning out the first few pieces. This extra lot cost will be in the price, if your supplier knows how to figure. Also, you should add the cost of scheduling and following the order. In essence, compute a realistic cost for setup. Think beyond our accepted definition.

Using a higher and more correct cost of setup will cause you to increase order quantities. Hence inventories. On the plus side, you will reduce the number of shop orders and setups. So you will save some machine capacity, scrap, Production Control, and other overhead costs.

Kardex record

Having determined lot sizes, many companies place orders accordingly. These may be for purchasing or for manufacturing. Their timing is often initiated by a perpetual inventory card file. On this may be kept records of Orders, Receipts, Issues, and back on Hand. This portrays a single Kardex card. In a regular file, you would see the lower margins of all cards in a file drawer, perhaps 100.

On such a card, you can record you economical lot size. This is suggested by the amount 150 written beside the title Ordered. With two such amounts, you can institute a manual control that signals at that stock level to reorder and how many.

Such a stock control may be used for raw materials, purchased parts, or finished stock-parts and end-products. Usually, it is operated to maintain inventories of parts-purchased and fabricated. In this process, reorders are often issued as routinely as minimums are reached. This is the method some companies get computers to carry out.

Inject Judgement

Assuming you aren't about to install a computer, I have two variations of a routine to recommend. Both call for injecting judgment between the signal that the minimum is reached and the actual reordering.

One procedure is like that carried on in a Newark, New Jersey, plant. Each morning a group assembled for a kaffeeklatsch. Present were representatives of Engineering, Purchasing, Manufacturing, and Production Control departments. These men heard each of the part numbers called out that had been removed from the Kardex file because a reorder point had been reached. About one, the Buyer might say, "That's made of brass. We'd better raise the quantity." About another, the Engineer might design." In this way, each unusual time had its quantity adjusted. All others followed a routine.

Another procedure is to classify items to separate routine handling from review. Cards could be coded, for instance, to indicate A, B or C degrees of activity. In contrast, they might be classified to call up for review all items that were subjected to peak and valley activities. In other works, you should use a routine reordering method as far as it is practical yet avoid its faults by applying special considerations to the unusual items.

Safety stock

Reorders are started by those who post withdrawals and see quantities drop to minimums established. An example is the 50 On Hand mentioned earlier.

Actually, such a minimum is made up of two quantities. One is the number you will need to carry on while replacements are coming through. The other is a cushion called safety stock. Its amount depends upon two factors. First is the likelihood of error in predicting your needs. Second is the promptness of customer service your company wishes to furnish.

These principles apply whether think of raw materials, purchased items, or finished stock. The differences are in lead times. How long doe sit take from the moment the signal is called to get what you customer wants to the shipping platform? This question promptly raises another. How close to your standard product is the one ordered? So you have degrees of special or standard. These determine what you must make to order and what you can carry in finished stock.

Service cost

When you consider putting final products on your shelves, again you must choose between alternatives. On the one hand are the costs of ownership. On the other are costs of profits you may lose. This latter factor is increasing. More pressures are being applied to force suppliers to carry customer's inventories and still provide prompt services.

Thus, the first decision is strategic. What do we mean by prompt service? Is that instantaneous, as the salesmen would have it? Or is it, As soon as we can get to it," the way the shop would like it? The point is that the amount of finished inventory you have to carry may head skyward as you approach instantaneous or 100 per cent service. To emphasize this cost, here are some percentages drawn from two sources, A and B.

The magnitude of increase in stock depends, of course, upon how regular you demand is, how closely you can predict that demand, and how quickly you can replace its withdrawal. As I state the answer, "The number you need on the shelf is the number you will sell in the time it takes to get them back on the shelf."

Seems simple enough. One is the wide range between peak and valley demand. Naturally, you have more protection against irregularly large demand when you are building inventory for the

Service per cent	Per cent inventory	
	A	B
75	100	100
90	129	220
99	177	628

peak. At the same time, unfortunately, you are lengthening your lead time for getting other products.

Three Choices

Hence, your choices are (1) to increase inventory; (2) to lengthen delivery promises, or (3) to choose which customers to disappoint.

For instance, I do no agree with the "24-hour service" promised by one company in Philadelphia. Certainly, the principle behind its stated policy is competitively excellent. But trying to keep this promise costs a lot profit in peak seasons. The extra costs could be reduced, I'm sure, if this company were to distinguish between regular customers and those who call because they can't get such service elsewhere.

Still, I grant that their loss of profit may be less expensive than sales efforts expended to get these new customers. Some much depends upon whether or not they are retained after the peak season. Also, of course, how profitable their continuing purchases turn out to be.

Define "enough"

Keep in mind, then, that maintaining enough stock is a complex straddling procedure. Basically, you need an understandable, preferably a numerical, definition of "enough." An example might be "sufficient stock to enable us to ship 90 per cent of our regular orders complete within X days." Some such policy is a necessary antidote for the periodic, irrational, spasmodic cry, "Our inventory is too high." More than that, deciding how often to disappoint you customers is a major determinant of size of inventory you must maintain. It shoots up geometrically as you attempt to approach perfect service.

Finally, achievement of shipment on time is the primary measure of Production Control effectiveness. Therefore, you must establish a yardstick that prescribes what is meant by "on time." Until you have a bench mark to go by, you will hear too many unjustified criticisms, of "late shipment." With this noisy wail in our ears, let's turn our attention toward shipping more promptly.

•

8 Basic Principles of Inventory Control

The role of sales forecasting in inventory control

We have had occasion to refer to the role of inventory a number of times already in this book, and specifically we have suggested that the degree of control which is exercised over the levels of inventory held within a marketing logistics system is a key influence on the reliability of product supply within the system. That is to say, inventory control is primarily concerned with ensuring that stocks of a company's products are made available on a consistent basis in the light of the company's service policy to its markets and the behaviour of market demand. The major part of this chapter is concerned with describing and illustrating the basic principles of inventory control in the context of differing assumptions regarding knowledge about demand, and the lead time between placing an order for stock replenishment and actually receiving the order. In one or two instances we shall assume perfect knowledge about demand in order to more effectively portray a concept, but in reality this situation is extremely rare. In fact, we can distinguish between different classes of knowledge about demand in the future, in accordance with familiar decision theory practice. It does not happen often that a decision maker, whether he is concerned about sales planning or inventory control, is either completely ignorant about future demand, or has perfect knowledge of future demand levels. We can think of one or two situations, perhaps, in which these conditions might apply: for example, the demand for a completely new type of product may not be known at all, though it would be a foolish company which would market such a product without any prior research into consumer attitudes and behaviour. At the other extreme, that of certainty, demand may be known as the result of contracted supplies to a known and defined market.

In general, therefore, knowledge regarding future demand falls into the category of either risk or uncertainty, depending upon the decision maker's ability to assess the probabilities associated with a range of demand levels occurring in the future. Clearly, an awareness of the probability distribution of demand is a considerable asset in the planning of inventory requirements, since this enables a company to minimise the number of times when either too much or too little stock is held. At the other end of the scale, a complete ignorance of demand in the future means that either inventory will be insufficient to satisfy high demand levels or the company will invest in huge inventory resources, much of which will be wasted. And since inventory costs a great deal of money, about which we shall have much to say later on in this chapter, it is evident that an accurate assessment of future demand is necessary in order to ensure that inventory investment within the marketing logistics system is kept to a minimum within the framework of the service policy adopted by the company.

Responsibility or the control of inventory therefore requires not only an awareness of how demand is likely to behave in the future, but also an understanding of some of the more familiar techniques of sales forecasting. Of course, inventory planning is aided by stability in the sales pattern, since a high degree of variability in future demand necessitates a higher level of inventory in order to minimise stock-out occurrences and thus meet the required service level. Therefore forecasting needs to identify not only the basic trend of sales into the future, but also the probability of particular variations in sales around this basic trend.

Sales forecasting involves essentially a combination of two elements, prediction and forecasting, and it is important to understand the difference between them. Prediction implies the anticipation of changes in the future, and literally mean a 'saying beforehand', whereas forecasting involves the projection of past performance into the future. It is important to recognise that forecasting is not an 'either one or the other' exercise, but rather a blend of both the predictive and forecasting aspects; indeed the selection of a particular approach depends on many factors, such as indeed the availability and relevance of past data, the degree of accuracy required, the length of time to be forecast, the importance of the forecast to the company, and so on. A further difference of approach in sales forecasting is where a distinction is made between the 'top-down' and 'bottom-up' approaches. The 'top-down' approach is essentially a macro approach to forecasting, and starts at the broadest level, that is with a forecast of future economic performance, whereas the 'bottom-up' approach is based on the anticipated requirements of individual consumers, and is therefore more of a micro approach.

An example may illustrate the two approaches more clearly: Let us suppose that an oil company wishes to forecast its future sales over a predetermined time period. Adopting the 'top-down' approach, the starting-point would be a forecast of gross national product as a measure of national economic performance. The rate of growth of the economy will influence energy requirements, and this will be the next level to be forecast. Next comes the forecast for the particular product group with which the company is concerned, and in order to arrive at this estimate, other competing sources of energy supply need to be analyzed, for example coal, natural gas, nuclear energy, etc. The final stage in the 'top-down' approach requires an assessment of the competitive environment within the oil industry in order for the oil company to derive a forecast of its own market share, and therefore its own likely sales.

The 'bottom-up' approach starts with the smallest unit in the market, the individual consumer, and the forecast of future sales is built up from estimates by each salesman of the business he expects to secure from each of his customers, both existing and potential. The figures for each sales territory are then consolidated by area or region, and perhaps modified at this stage to allow for certain variables, which have not been considered at the sales territory level, to be taken into account. Such factors might include knowledge of anticipated changes in company policy or of forthcoming promotional campaigns likely to affect sales in the future. Finally, regional forecasts are aggregated into a company forecast, again with adjustments made where appropriate.

It would be optimistic to expect the final forecasts from the two approaches to coincide, since they are derived in totally different ways - one is aggregative, the other disaggregative, and unless care is taken, much accuracy may be lost either way. Good forecasting require an appreciation of the merits and limitations of both approaches, and the techniques within each approach, and attempts to reconcile between the different results achieved. There is no *a priori* basis upon which to select any one technique in preference to the others, and, as we have said, selection of the most appropriate forecasting methodology is dependent upon the context within which the forecast is to be made.

A particular method of forecasting sales which is popular for inventory control purposes is the exponential smoothing technique, because of its great economy from a data processing viewpoint. For a company dealing with a large range of products, a technique which reduces the costs of forecasting with respect to data handling has considerable advantage over other methods requiring the manipulation of extensive series of data. Exponential smoothing is a forecasting technique of great simplicity: it emphasizes the difference between the most recent forecast and-the latest observation in order to arrive at a new forecast. There is a certain logic in developing a new forecast on the basis of the degree of error present in the most recent forecast. However, it is necessary to decide to what extent such error should be accounted for in the preparation of a forecast. The basic formula for exponential smoothing is:

New forecast = $x\%$ Old forecast + $y\%$ latest demand observation, where $x + y = 100$.

The weighting factor for the latest demand observation, that is for actual demand is the latest or most recent period, is commonly symbolized by α. Using a suitable notation for the other terms in the formula, we obtain:

$$Fn = (1 - \alpha) f_0 + \lambda$$

where fn = new forecast

f_o = old forecast

λ = latest demand observation

The formula may be rewritten as

$$f_n = f_0 + \alpha\,(\lambda - f_0)$$

Notice how the value of a affects the sensitivity and stability of the new forecast. Clearly, if a is given a value of 1, $fn = \lambda$, thus making the new forecast maximally sensitive to latest data, and highly unstable over time. At one other extreme, if α is given a value of 0, $fn = f_0$, and the new forecast is extremely stable over time yet at the same time totally insensitive. In practice, a is usually given a value of around 0.1, which, for monthly sales forecasting, corresponds to a moving average of 19 months' demand, and rarely exceeds 0.3. To illustrate the application and effect of the exponential smoothing method on a series of sales figures, a value for a of 0.1 is contrasted with a value of 0.7, and the results are shown in Table 5.1. With a = 0.1, fn is very stable over time, but is relatively insensitive to actual demand. With a = 0.7, fn is relatively unstable, but reasonably sensitive to the latest demand figures. In fact, in our example, the higher a value gives a better estimate than the lower value, but this would have to be tested over a longer period of time. The choice of the most appropriate a value is largely a matter of judgment, though the characteristics of demand and the degree of randomness is particular should be given special attention.

The costs of inventory in marketing logistics systems

Inventory management is indeed a central activity in marketing logistics planning and control, as shown in Wendell Stewart's description of activity 'cogs' in a distribution system. Inventory has been described as the meat in the sandwich between production and sales, and represents an area of potential conflict between the two functions; the production manager prefers constant production runs in order to cut costs, whilst the sales manager would like immediate inventory availability to service variable customer demands. Production would like to build up inventory at a constant rate to suit specific economic requirements, in contrast with sales management's desire to draw from inventory in accordance with market demand. It is clearly important to get to grips, therefore, with the basic concepts of inventory control, and to understand how costs are incurred in maintaining inventory for the purposes of offering a service to the market.

Inventory has obvious trade-off potential; if a company had production facilities immediately adjoining all its customers, little inventory would be required; however, the 'discrepancy of assortments' between a company and its customers imposes movement and storage obligations on the company, and these, as we have seen, are prime candidate areas for trade-off analysis. Later in this chapter, we shall explore a method for assessing the amount of inventory investment required in multi-item situations—at this stage it is pertinent to mention the role of ABC analysis under these conditions. We referred earlier to ABC analysis as a means of ranking products according to their profitability, or contribution to sales revenue, and incorporated with it Critical Value Analysis in order to reflect the service performance required from each product. By this method, some products are identified as being priority products, and policy may be to locate them as near to the market as possible, say at regional field warehouses: these may be classified as A-group products. B-group products may require inventory placement at, say, a central warehouse adjacent to the factory, whilst C-group products may not be inventoried in warehouses, but may be produced as required. The reason why such a selective approach to inventory control in multi-item situations in required is the high costs involved in carrying inventory. It is to the nature of inventory costs, therefore, that we now turn our attention.

The analysis of inventory is essentially one in which different types of cost are balanced, or traded off against one another. There are three main types of cost with which the inventory manager is concerned, *ordering costs, carrying costs* and *stockout costs.* In order to explain them, we shall assume we are dealing with one particular part of the total marketing logistics system, namely a field warehouse placed between the factory and a group of customers serviced from that warehouse. Our analysis will be concerned with the development of basic procedures for the replenishment of warehouse inventory from the factory. The principles expounded here are directly applicable to other areas of inventory management, such as the control of inventory at a central factory-based location or at retail stores.

Ordering costs are those costs associated with expediting an order placed by the warehouse on the factory. The basic cost areas to be included are order transmission costs, order processing costs incurred in internal administrative departments and at relevant receiving an despatch bays, and possible production 'set-up' costs if the order cannot be met out of inventory. In a number of cases, the total of these costs may not vary significantly from one order to the next, and in simple inventory control procedures, a fixed cost per order is often assumed.

Inventory carrying costs are frequently given inadequate attention in assessing total inventory costs. This is because of the common failure to recognize inventory as an idle, though economic, resource; a company, in carrying a certain level of inventory is actually investing capital which is tied up inside warehouses. It is therefore appropriate to apply an opportunity cost factor in the compilation of overall inventory carrying costs to reflect the fact that capital is being tied up which could otherwise be employed elsewhere inside the organization. Such a cost factor should take into account the potential earning power of the capital which is being foregone. This should certainly be not less than the current rate of interest on money, and, depending on the circumstances of the company, may range up to 20-25 per cent, or more. Besides capital costs, other carrying costs include what may be broadly defined as inventory risk costs, covering such areas as stock deterioration and obsolescence, and insurance charges; and the actual costs of the warehouse space used, which may be the rent charged in the case of public warehousing, or all the costs involved in operating a company-owned Generally, risk and storage costs represent no more than about 5 per cent of the value of a product, and therefore, bearing in mind the high opportunity cost element, it is clear that a reduction in inventory investment would have a significant impact on inventory costs in terms of the amount of capital which would thereby be released for investment elsewhere.

Stockout costs, reflect the cost incurred by a company as the result of being out of stock when an order is placed by customers. In our example, three possible actions are available to a customer who places an order on the warehouse and is met with an out-of-stock situation. He may choose to wait until the inventory is replenished or until a special backorder is completed on his behalf: this would be his normal reaction, but a small cost is likely because of the special nature of the order. Alternatively, the customer may withdraw the order, which would represent a higher cost to the company, or, more costly still, he may withdraw entirely his patronage of the company. Clearly, in those cases where stockouts do occur, the actual costs involved are difficult to assess, but a simple procedure for estimating these costs will be presented later in the chapter.

The main decisions facing the inventory manager are *how much* to order and *when* to order for inventory replenishment in order to minimise costs under a given service policy. An alternative approach which we shall also consider is the development of an optimum service policy given a knowledge of inventory costs.

Categories of inventory and inventory policy

In order to answer the questions of how much and when to order, we need to know more about the nature of inventory within a marketing logistics system. We can distinguish between three types of inventory, or stock: *in-transit stock, base stock,* and *safety stock.* In-transit stock refers to inventory in the pipeline', and represents the total amount of inventory moving through the distribution system at any point in time. Average in-transit stock levels are simply calculate by multiplying average demand per time period by the stock transit time between fixed system facilities. In the case of inventory movement between a factory and a warehouse, the average transit time between which is three days, average in-transit stock for a demand level of 100 units per six-day week equals units, or 50 units.

Base stock represents the amount of inventory required to meet the average level of demand during average lead time. Lead time is the total time involved between the placement of an order for inventory replenishment, and the receipt, of the inventory into the warehouse, and is therefore made up of transportation, order processing and order transmission times. Where demand is known and constant, and where lead time is fixed, then base stock represents the total amount of inventory required for servicing demand. However, such conditions are usually exceptional, and normally an extra amount of inventory is required in order to cover variations from the average level of demand and average lead time: this extra amount of inventory is known as safety, or buffer, stock. Calculation of base stock requirements is relatively easy-if average lead time is, say, two weeks, then a base stock of 200 units is needed, given an average demand of 100 units per week. Safety stock levels are more complex to determine, and are, of course, dependent upon how much cover the company wishes to provide for itself with respect to the variations in demand and lead time; in other words, they depend upon the policy which the company wishes to adopt regarding service level. If a company adopts a service level of 95 per cent, we may interpret this as meaning that it is prepared to accept a stockout percentage of 5 per cent- that is, on five occasions out of every 100, it will be out of stock. It is in such a situation that the accuracy of sales forecasting has particular relevance. The following example illustrates this.

Company A has specified a service level policy of 97.5 per cent, that is, it is prepared to accept stockouts occurring on average on five occasions out of every 200 orders placed by customers. The forecasted demand for the next 48 weeks is as follows:

> 15, 25, 25, 10, 15, 15, 25, 25, 20, 20, 10, 15, 15, 5, 10, 15, 20, 20, 15, 20, 20, 30, 20, 25, 15, 20, 10, 10, 15, 10, 15, 25, 35, 20, 10, 10, 5, 15, 15, 10, 15, 20, 20, 30, 20, 10, 5, 5.

Lead time is fixed at one week for stock replenishment at the company's field warehouse, from which all demand is to be met. In order to assess the amount of base stock needed, we calculate the average level of demand per week, which is the relevant lead time period; this is approximately 17 units. We see that, as is typical in the analysis of demand, the forecasted sales per week are *normally distributed* around the mean level of demand of 17 units: that is, a frequency distribution of demand results in the familiar bell-shaped curve characteristic of the normal distribution common in statistical analysis. The standard deviation of demand is approximately seven units, and can be approximated by multiplying the mean absolute deviation by 1.25. The mean absolute deviation is simply the sum of all deviations from the mean, ignoring sign, and dividing by the number of observations. Within the two vertical lines spanning lead time, a service of demand alternatives is shown. A continuation of the past levels of demand, or withdrawals from inventory, is shown by the heavy line. Zero demand during lead time is shown as a, and a demand level which creates a stockout situation is shown as d; b and c represent demand levels between these two extremes. The service level policy of 97.5 per cent permits a stockout percentage of 2.5 per cent, and the shaded area represents that portion of the area under the normal curve within which demand cannot be satisfied from inventory, as no inventory is available. Reference to statistical tables of the normal distribution function indicates that 95 per cent of the area under a normal curve is contained within + 1.96 standard deviations from the mean. Since we are not concerned with the left-hand tail of the normal distribution, it is clearr that 97.5 per cent of demand will be met within 1.96 standard deviations from the mean along the right-hand side of the normal distribution, leaving 2.5 per cent as the stockout percentage. With a standard deviation of 7 units, the required safety stock is therefore 14 units, or 1.96 standard deviations of lead time demand.

Our example thus generates a base stock requirement of 17 units, and safety stock of 14 units at the specified level, which, taken together, indicate the level of inventory at which an order for replenishment should be made. That is, the inventory re-order point is given by summing base stock and safety stock requirements. Where a company operates a number of inventory points, it is possible to estimate the total safety stock level at the *n* locations, given the safety stock requirements at one location. This is shown as a generalized relationship:

$$SSn = SS1\ (n)\ \sqrt{n}$$

Where SS_n = safety stock at n locations

SS_1 = safety stock at one location

n = number of location

Base stock is not involved in the increase in inventory since it is unaffected by the increase in the number of inventory points. The formula above indicates that total safety stock tends to increase, but at a diminishing rate, with respect to the number of locations. The relationship is a guideline only, since clearly the market area served by each inventory point has unique, individual demand characteristics, requiring separate safety stock calculations.

There are two principal types of inventory policy open to the inventory manager. The *fixed order quantity* policy is characterized by (1) an order quantity which remains constant over time, that is there is no variation in the size of the order placed for stock replenishment: (2) a variable re-order period, which in the time period which elapses between, the placing of each order; and (3) a constant re-order point. The heavy vertical lines represent the fixed order size, and the actual time when orders are placed is clearly dependent upon the movement of inventory relative to the re-order point. By way of contrast, the *fixed re-order period* policy has time as the influencing variable on ordering policy—its major characteristics are (1) a re-order period which is constant over time, that is the time interval between orders is fixed; (2) variable re-order points—this is a logical consequence of a fixed re-order period except under conditions of extreme stability and regularity in demand; and (3) an order quantity which varies from one order to the next. The two policies are often referred to as Q-system and P-system policies respectively.

Q-system policies require the determination of what is usually known as an *economic order quantity*, and this is arrived at by reference to the costs involved in ordering and carrying inventory.

Under the P-system policy, however, the order quantity is derived either as the result of a short-term demand forecast, or by subtracting the inventory level at the re-order time from some desired maximum level. We shall explore these different policies at some length in the next section. At a more general level, however, we can list a number of features of the two systems which may help the inventory manager to decide which particular system to adopt. No one system is *per se* preferable to the other—each must be weighed up and reviewed in the light of individual logistics requirements. As a general guideline, then, we should recognise the following broad features.

The fixed re-order period policy usually requires accurate short-term demand forecasting—under some circumstances, particularly if demand is volatile, this may be difficult to achieve. However, under conditions of high demand instability, a fixed order quantity policy may lead to higher inventory levels.

Under most conditions, however, the fixed order quantity policy carries a lower level of inventory, thus lowering carrying costs.

If there are sudden changes in demand, the fixed re-order period policy fails to provide an automatic response because it is time-department. Q system policies are more responsive because they are demand-dependent.

In trading off inventory management decisions against transportation decisions, vehicles scheduling requirements need to be taken into account. If strict vehicle scheduling is necessary in order to keep transportation costs down, then a P-system policy may be required.

Because Q-system policies are demand-dependent, inventory needs to be more closely watched, and where a large number of items is involved this may be a costly exercise.

Before we look in detail at a number of inventory policies under varying demand conditions, we examine the single-order situation, where the problem of when to order does not arise.

Inventory control in the single order situation

The inventory policies which we outlined above are based upon the usual requirement to place a number of orders for stock replenishment over a period of time. This lead us to consider procedures for determining not only how much to order each time, but when to place each order. However, not all inventory problems are of this type. Consider the case of the retail fashion house faced with the need to order a batch of dresses which will sell for a limited period only; we may represent this as a single-order inventory problem. Or consider the decision facing the supermarket manager of how many cases of bananas to order each week in order to maximise his profits; in this situation, a similar issue arises. The problem is how much to order, say, each Saturday for the following week's trading. Each example may be classified as a single-order inventory problem over a given time period. A solution procedure is given below with reference to the second example, but which is directly applicable to the first type of situation.

The supermarket manager must decide how many bananas to order from his wholesaler for the coming week. He has regularly bought a certain number of cases each week, and sells some or all of them. The supermarket makes a profit on those cases sold, but a loss is incurred on those cases which remain unsold and which can be returned at the end of the week. We assume that bananas which are purchased for one week's trading cannot be sold in the following week. The demand for bananas in the store varies from one week to the next, but an analysis of past sales will enable the supermarket manager to determine the probabilities of selling specified numbers of cases each week. A subjective assessment of future demand relative to the historical trend should also be carried out. This problem is essentially a normative, stochastic decision problem which can readily be expressed in mathematical terms.

The first step is to identify the relevant variables, which are as follows:

N	=	the number of cases ordered per week
ϕ	=	the profit per case
λ	=	the loss per returned case
D	=	the weekly demand
$p(D)$	=	probability that demand = D any one week
π	=	profit per week.

The problem is to identify the optimum value for N so that the expected profit per week is maximised: since demand probabilities are known, the problem is a fairly simple decision one under conditions of risk. By taking into account the probabilities associated with different demand levels above and below the number of cases ordered.

By inputting different values for N within the appropriate demand range, the N value which produces the highest expected profit should be chosen as the order size. For example, the expected profit on an order of three cases of bananas is as follows, where profit per case sold is £3.00, loss per returned case is £1.50, and demand ranges from 1 to 5 cases with probabilities of 0.1, 0.2, 0.4, 0.2 and 0.1, for demand for 1,2,3,4 and 5 cases respectively:

: = 0.1 {(1 x £3) — (£1.50 x 2)} + 0.2 {(2 x £3) — £1.50 x 1) + 0.4 (3 x £3) + 0.2(3 x £3) + 0.1 (3 x :3) —£7.20

This produces an expocted profit which is higher for N = 3 than for any other value of N within the range 1 to 5, and therefore the order and quantity should be set at 3 cases. It must be remembered, however, that significant changes in demand should be monitored in terms of their impact on the optimum order quantity—a substantial-shift in the demand probabilities would lead to a different optimum order quantity.

Demand certainty and the optimum order quantity

We now turn our attention to the development of procedures for determining the optimum order quantity and optimum re-order point in situations where re-ordering takes place. To begin with, we shall assume conditions of demand certainty, that is there exists perfect knowledge regarding the future behaviour of demand, and of a fixed lead time. We shall then relax these assumptions by allowing variability in both demand and lead time: this will lead us to modify our calculations for optimum order quantity, in order to account for the costs of running out of stock. Since fixed re-order period policies are generally more complex to develop and not as common in application, our emphasis will be on Q-system policies.

Under conditions of demand certainty and fixed lead time, when to order is a straightforward decision. It is determined with reference to base stock only, there being no safety stock requirements because variability has been assumed away. Thus, the re-order point should be set at that level of inventory which just covers lead time demand. How much to order, however, must be determined with reference to ordering and carrying costs. Ordering costs and carrying costs generally move in opposite directions as a function of order size and therefore as a function of the number of order placed. In the first situation, an order quantity of 80 units generates an average inventory level of 40 units, but only three orders are needed over the period. In the second situation, an order quantity of 40 units reduces average inventory to 20 units, but raises ordering costs because of the greater number of orders required. In situation(a), inventory carrying costs are higher than in (b), but ordering costs are lower. If we assume inventory carrying costs to be £1 per unit, and ordering costs constant at £10 per order, the total of the two costs under (a) is £70, and under (b) £80. Therefore, an order quantity of 80 units per order is more economic than one of 40 units. However, we have compared only two alternative order quantities: is there an order quantity which is more economic than 80 units? In fact, what is the optimum economic order quantity? A simple formula, known as the EOQ formula, enables us to calculate the answer.

Firstly, we identify with symbols the variables pertinent to the problem; these are as follows:

Q = economic order quantity (EOQ)

A = ordering costs per order

S = annual sales

i = annual carrying costs per unit

TC = total inventory costs

The number of orders per year is given by S/Q^*, and therefore total ordering costs are equal to $A(S/Q^*)$. Average inventory is given by $Q^*/2$, and therefore total carrying costs equal i $(Q^*/2)$. By adding the two costs together, we obtain:

$$TC = A(S/Q^*) + i(Q^*/2)$$

The optimum value of Q^* is easily calculated by differential calculus. The total cost equation may be rewritten as

$$TC = ASQ^{*1} = \frac{1}{2} iQ^*$$

Differentiating TC with respect to Q^*, and setting to zero, we obtain:

$$\frac{dTC}{dQ^*} = —ASQ^{*-2} + \frac{1}{2} i = 0$$

$$ASQ^{*-2} = \tfrac{1}{2}i$$

Solving for Q^*, we have $Q^* = \sqrt{2AS/i}$, which is the classical *EOQ* formula.

Application of the formula to our example, with an annual demand of 1000 units, gives an *EOQ* of approximately 142 units. Thus, we have found out how much to order each time in order to minimise inventory ordering and carrying costs. Under constant demand and lead time conditions, when to order is, as we mentioed earlier, dictated by the lead time; if lead time is two weeks, then re-ordering should take place when enough inventory is available to just cover two weeks' demand. The number of times re-ordering takes place is simply computed; it is equal to S/Q^*, which, in our example, is equal to approximately 7 times.

Although EOQ has its limitations in assuming no variability in demand and lead time and no stockouts, it is relatively insensitive to changes in the input values. For example, if demand were as much as 1200 units, and not 1000 as forecast, the economic order quantity would rise by only 13 units, to 155. Therefore, if actual demand were 20 per cent higher than forecast, the error in EOQ would only be about 9 per cent. The difference in total costs is even less significant. With an order quantity of 142 units calculated as optimum on a forecast of 1000, total inventory costs for an actual sales level of 1200 are £156. If sales had been forecast correctly, the economic order quantity of 155 would have generated total inventory costs of

£155. This versatility of performance relative to input values is the major reason why EOQ is so popular as a method of inventory control.

Optimum order quantity and re-order point under risk

Given variability in demand and lead time, it is clear that a major problem facing inventory management is that of ascertaining when and how much to order so that the risk of running out of stock is consonant with service policy. This problem reduces to one of calculating a safety level for inventory in the light of known or forecast variations in demand and lead time from average levels. Let us assume that, on the basis of both historical data and subjective judgment, the management of the XYZ Manufacturing Company is able to attach probabilities to the time it takes for an order placed by the warehouse manager to be received at the warehouse to replenish inventory. Likewise, estimates can also be made of the probability of demand in units per day. It is a relatively simple matter to translate the data into demand probabilities during lead time. For example, the probability that 6 units will be demanded during lead time is given as:

$$P\text{ (6 units)} = P\text{ (lead time = 2 days)} \times P\text{(3 units per day)} \times P\text{(3 units per day)}$$
$$= (0.2)\ (0.3)\ (0.3) = 0.018$$

Table XYZ Manufacturing Co-probability estimates for lead time and demand

Lead Time	*Probability*	*Demand*	*Probability*
2 days	0.2 units	3 units	0.3
3 days	0.6	4 units	0.7
4 days	0.2		

The probability that 7 units will be demanded during lead time is:

P(7 units) = {p(led time = 2 days x P(3 units per day) x

p(4 units per day) + {P lead time = 2 days) x
P(4 units per day) x P(3 units per day)}
= {(0.2) (0.3) (0.7)} + {(0.2) (0.7) (0.3)} = 0.084

The minimum level of demand during lead time is clearly 6 units and the maximum level is 16 units. Similar computations for the probabilities of all possible demand levels between 6 and 16 result in a table of demand probabilities during lead time. If the XYZ Manufacturing Company set its re-order point at 16 units, no stockouts would occur. However, holding maximum inventory is expensive in terms of inventory carrying costs, and is tantamount to providing a service policy of 100 per cent. Let us assume that the company has decided to operate a service policy of 87 per cent, which is equivalent to permitting a stockout percentage of 13 per cent. The company should therefore set its inventory re-order point at 14 units for an 87 per cent service level. Whenever the warehouse inventory falls to 14 units, an order should be placed for stock replenishment. The question now facing XYZ Manufacturing Company is: how much should be ordered each time? We shall approach this problem by considering firstly the costs involved in actually running out of stock.

Table. XYZ Manufacturing Co-demand probabilities during lead time

Demand during lead time (x units)	*Probability*	*Probability that Demond > x units**
6	0.01800	0.98200
7	0.08400	0.89800
8	0.09800	0.80000
9	0.01620	0.78380
10	0.11340	0.67040
11	0.26460	0.40580
12	0.20742	0.19838
13	0.01512	0.18326
14	0.05292	0.13034
15	0.08232	0.04802
16	0.04802	0.00000
	1,00000	

We argued earlier that, broadly speaking, there are three possible consequences of not being able to satisfy an order from inventory—a backorder may take place, the order may be lost, or the customer may be lost. If XYZ management were able to determine average costs associated with each possibility, then these costs coupled with estimates of the probability of each event occurring would generate an expected stockout cost. The Table represents the expected cost per stockout calculated by the XYX manufacturing Company, and is simply the sum of the product of the probability of each event occurring and the relevant cost estimate. Given an expected stockout cost of £ 10 per order, the stockout cost of a service policy of 87 per cent is therefore given by multiplying the stockout percentage of 13 per cent by the stockout cost. This is equal to a stockout cost per order of £1.30.

9 Controlling Stocks

The financial investment tied up in total manufacturing stocks is bound to represent a very high proportion of the capital employed in any typical manufacturing company. Total inventory comprises purchased materials and work in progress. The value of work in progress includes not only the relevant materials costs, but also the value added in terms of labour costs incurred in machining, assembly and all the other process operations throughout the factory. Stocks and work in progress away on subcontractors' premises also contribute to this total investment. Since so much capital is attributable to inventory holding, it follows that sensible and efficient control of stock levels is an essential ingredient of profitable management.

For a given level of factory output, the value of work in progress must depend largely on the average throughput time taken by work through the plant. Put very crudely, a factory with an average throughput time of three months would probably carry about twice the amount of work in progress as another factory making the same product, at the same rate, but with a throughput of six weeks. Thus efficient production control and materials movement between workstations is obviously another very important factor. Since production control and plant layout are important elements in the control of work in progress.

Distribution managers rightly take a wider view of total inventory costs because their responsibility extends to goods in warehouses and other premises off site, and in vehicles and vessels plying between those places. These distribution aspects are complex, and solving the problem of providing good customer service while avoiding excessive stock levels and transport costs becomes a challenging exercise in logistics.

In this chapter we are concerned with the control of stocks in the factory stores. Although there may be a person in the organisation with the title 'stock controller', in reality the management of local stock levels in a team function involving the purchasing, involving the purchasing, stores, stock control and production control personnel.

Stock records

First, however, it fairly obvious that no control over stock levels can be exercised at all unless a firm knows, with reasonable accuracy, the actual levels of stocks held at all times. All records systems cost money to operate, whether of stocks held at all times. All records systems cost money to operate, whether they are carried out manually or by computer. It is useful to consider the classes of stock items according to the financial value that each represents, in order that systems and management attention can be concentrated on the most significant items.

ABC stock classification

Using Pareto's rule as a basis, stock can be considered in three categories, *A*, *B* and *C*. The Pareto's rule demonstrates that a high proportion of stock value is represented by a relatively small number of high-cost stock items. These can be called the *A* items, which demand the highest level of attention. At the other end of the scale, large numbers of small components, such as nuts, screws and washers, warrant only some simple form of recording and control: these are the C items. The remaining B items will need to be recorded in a stock level system - most probably the same system as the A items - but there will not be the same urgency to keep strict control over ordering levels and timing.

Basic stock record information

Many stock record systems depend on index cards, the information on which is entered and updated as stores inputs and issues occur. In the past such systems were duplicated in the stores and in the stock control departments and where such duplicated or triplicated sets of records existed it was always a fairly safe bet that no two sets of records would ever agree exactly. This is one area where a centralised computer can prove really useful, with terminals located in the stores and purchasing departments that allow information to be updated immediately stock movements take place. Whatever system is used, and whether it is clerical or computer based, the following data are usually required for each stock item.

A code number

Must be unique to the particular stock item, which allows the item to be identified without ambiguity for all purposes. This code may well be allocated to fit in with the firm's own drawing numbering system, or the costing system, or both of these.

Description

Used in conjunction with the code number for identification. This may include a summary of technical data for purchased components. Descriptions are necessary as back-up identification, to avoid expensive mistakes when clerks make copying errors when writing down long code numbers. Descriptions are also obviously vital when the code number has been forgotten or is not known.

Quantity held in stock

A function of movements into and out of stock. It is usual to record these movements in addition to the actual residual stock quantity. Where issues are made, details of relevant job numbers are entered; when new stock arrives the particular batch quantity is entered together with the purchase order number.

Stores location or bin number

A coded address that positively indicates the rack,

shelf, bin or other location where the item is normally stored.

Stock control information

Includes planned maximum and minimum stock quantities, the stock level at which re-ordering should take place, and so on.

Cost data

Typically, such costs are computed and entered afresh for each new intake batch. However, in standard consisting system, such entries are used to assist the accounts department in calculating historical variances and in setting up periodically new standard cost levels.

Selling price

This is occasionally needed, especially where stock lists are generated for issue to sales staff, or where the stores is actually responsible for handling and invoicing customer's orders.

Issue restrictions

May include the reservation of certain stocks for particular jobs. Recording such information in the stores record system can prevent the inadvertent issue of stocks that are required against some other vital need .

There is probably no such thing as typical stock record card, because systems vary greatly from one company to another.

Computerised stock records

Stock record systems and computers are a logical

combination. Using the stock code number as the principal identifier for each item, it is a straightforward job to set up a database. Once this has been done, computer terminals in the stores and in related departments can be used to interrogate the database at any time, and fresh information on stock movements or the issue or purchase orders for replacement stocks can be fed into the system. without delay.

Once a stock database has been set up, the computer can be made to produce reports which are edited or sequenced to suit a number of different departments in the factory. These could include a listing of all stocks, sorted according a stock numbers or by an alphabetical sorting of the first character in the description. Where, for example, retail prices are printed out alongside all items, stocklists become valuable to salesmen and others who detail directly with taking customer orders. A large 'mainframe' computer is not always required, and minicomputers can often cope.

Stock movements

It is useful to stop at this point and list various ways and means by which stocks can be added or subtracted from stores holdings. *Inputs* can arrive in stores through three main routes. These are:

1 Receipts from outside suppliers, documented into stores by means of goods inwards inspection notes, or simply by reference to the particular purchase order number.

2 Components manufactured within the factory released by inspection notes or by an

inspector's stamp against the final operation on the relevant batch route card

3 Goods returned to stores as surplus to factory production requirements. It is useful to pass such returns through the inspection department in order that inspection dockets can be issued which clarify that the goods are fit for re-issue.

Outputs can happen through:

1 Issue to the factory, either against requisitions or against instructions constrained in parts lists or raw materials lists which accompany the appropriate works order.

2 Direct sales of finished goods to outside customers.

3 Management decisions to scrap or sell of redundant, surplus items.

If just one item of stock is considered over a long period, the quantity held must fluctuate in sympathy with stores receipts and issues. This leads in to some of the problems encountered in controlling stock levels.

Methods for controlling stock levels

The two-bin method

Low-cost items such as consumables may be suitable for stock control by the two-bin method. In the case of quantities of nuts, bolts, washers and other small parts the storekeeper has two bins for each item. One bin is used for issues and the other held in reserve. The issuing bin contains a travelling requisition is sent to the buyer for a suitable quantity to be reordered. The second, reserve, bin is then used for issues while the reorder quantity is awaited after which the first bin becomes the new reserve.

This method also works for stationery supplies. Consider a stock of letter head stationery on a shelf stored in boxes of one ream (500 sheets) each. If a travelling requisition is placed to protrude at a suitable level in a stack of boxes this will ensure re-ordering when the pile has been reduced to the minimum quantity allowable. The remainder of the pile then acts as a reserve whilst new deliveries are awaited.

Economic order quantity

Stocks for continuous or batch production are liable to be over-ordered because of the lure of quantity discounts. Against any advantage in lower prices obtained through bulk ordering must be the increased costs of storage, risk of obsolescence and the cost of capital employed. By comparing all the costs involved in carrying in inventory with purchase prices in relation to quantities, it is theoretically possible to produce a set of curves similar. These curves show that there is one particular order quantity where the advantages of quantity discount are just balanced by the increased costs of inventory carrying this quantity being regarded as the economic order quantity (EOQ) for the particular commodity under consideration.

In practice many other factors determine the actual quantity to be ordered. It may be, for example, that delivery times from suppliers are so long that high stocks must be held in order to avoid lost production time through stockouts. Also, it is generally recognised that considerable flexibility can be exercised in varying the amount ordered above or below the precise economic level. The curve representing total cost is usually above or below the precise economic level. The curve representing total cost is usually shallow around is lowest point and, provided on does not stray too far from the optimum quantity, differences in the amounts ordered will not have a great effect on the total unit cost.

The formulas ordered will not have a great effect on the total unit cost.

The annual fixed costs of acquisition are equal to the number of orders per year multiplied by the fixed cost per order.

$=DS/O$

where D = annual sales volume for the demand (units)

S = fixed cost per order (or setup costs for a manufactured batch)

O= order quantity (units)

The annual variable costs of possession aremonetary clue) multiplied by an inventory-carrying-cost, factor. This is multiplied by an inventory-carrying factor. This is

$1/2\ OVI$

Where V = cost per unit

I = (cost of carrying inventory)/

The annual total inventory service cost is at its lowest when the two are equal, which is when

$$DS/Q = 1/2\ QVI$$

Whence $Q^2 = 2DS/VI$

and $Q = (2DS/VI)$

EOQ example

Suppose that: D = 1000 units per year

S = £10 fixed cost per order

V = £4 per unit

I = 26% inventory carrying cost

Substituting in the formula we get:

$Q = 2 \times 1000 \times 10$

4×0.25

$Q = 20\ 000/11$

$= 141$ units

This would suggest seven orders per year.

In practice there is no need for many tedious calculation. There are many EOQ tables monographs available. EOQ theory will certainly not cope with every type of inventory problem. Its success depends, to a large extent, on a reasonably stable usage figure. Nevertheless, its application has given many firms considerable financial benefits.

Order levels and safety stocks

Consider the artificial situation in which production is started using an initial stock of a particular item, with reordering taking place at prearranged intervals so that the stock is replenished at precisely the correct economic time. Each order is placed for the economic quantity (EOQ) and orders are spaced so that the stockholding just falls to zero as the next supply arrives. By this approach the perfect condition is presented where the average amount of inventory held is kept to a minimum.

In practice, of course, the perfect situation can never occur. Many variables will wreck any attempt to achieve the perfect stock condition. These variables include:

1 Uneven stock usage for production

2 Unexpected wastage or losses

3 Failure by suppliers to maintain consistent delivery times

4 Goods received short or damaged from suppliers.

Some of these variations can be accommodated in planning . For example, seasonal fluctuations can often be predicted and allowed for. However, some safety factor must always be provided and this takes the form of safety stocks, sometimes called buffer stock-level and this illustrates the way in which buffer stocks safeguard against possible contingencies. The skill of the stock controller must be exercised in determining reorder levels and reorder quantities in order to achieve the planned maximum and minimum actual stockholdings.

The curve shows that, for the stock item being considered, 6000 units have been provided against a predicted usage rate of 1000 units per month. In other words, sufficient stocks have been laid in to cover the first six month of production. In order to safeguard against unforeseen contingencies a 'safety stock' of 2000 units has been planned. With the economic order quantity having been calculated at around 6000 units, the reorder point occurs when stocks fall to 4000 units for a supplier's lead time of two months.

In the diagram, it is apparent that all went a planned during the first 'stockcycle'. Usage took place at the predicted 1000 units per month, and an order was placed for 6000 fresh units when stocks fell to the planned reorder point of planned maximum level of 8000 units after the expected lead time of two months. The first 'unforeseen contingency' took place during the end of the second stock cycle, after the second replacement order had been placed: 1000 units were scrapped as a result of an operator's error during a guillotining process. The deficiency was immediately made good from safety stocks. During the third stock cycle, the supplier had a strike on his hands , with the result that his delivery time was extended to over three months, in place of the expected two. Again, the safety stocks were sufficient in this case to cover production requirements.

In the last stock cycle shown a small disaster has occurred. The stock controller, true to his instruction, has automatically placed an order for 6000 fresh stock items as soon as stocks sand to the 4000 re-order point. What the stock controller did not know, however,was that the product range on which his stock item was solely used had been discontinued. Production ceased only one month after the new batch of stock arrived, so that the surplus stocks were in fact redundant. The same thing happened to all the other stock items used solely on this particular product range and created a serious problem of redundant stocks. With any system he generates orders automatically for fresh stocks, safeguards must be rigidly applied to prevent mistakes of this expensive nature from happening. Every order must be questioned by a production of purchasing manager who has access to forward sales and production plans.

Determination of planned maximum, minimum and re-order stock levels must obviously start from the production plans. What may not be so obvious is that any change in these plans must be communicated immediately to those responsible for ordering stocks. Given a thorough and up-to-date knowledge of production requirements, the stock controller can apply a number of methods to arrive at re-order quantities, re-order points, and the theoretical safety stock levels that these quantities will produce.

Statistical determination of safety stock levels

For routine stock replacements, a commonly

applied method for setting safety stock levels is to arrange that these should approximate to one month's normal production requirements, or to half the stocks used during the purchase lead time, whichever is the greater. Naturally this rule-of-thumb approach can give rise to anomalies. It is arguable that the only true way to decide safety stock requirements is to consider all the possible variables, and then to adopt a statistical approach to arrive at levels that are reasonable in the context of the probability level of stock shortages which can be tolerated. This problem can be described in terms of 'service levels' where a 100 per cent level means that there is never any shortage of stocks when they are required. A 98 per ent service level would describe a situation where two out of every hundred application to the stores were met with an 'out of stock' reply. It is generally recognised that 100 per cent service levels, for many reasons, are difficult to achieve and would in fact be prohibitive in terms of inventory costs. The statistical approach, therefore, attempts to reconcile a conscious policy decision on adequate service levels with the amount of stock required to achieve those levels.

Once the realms of statistics are entered, mathematical solution beyond the understanding of most stock control clerks are encountered. The subject is complex, and the results will only be as good as the estimates of demand and the accuracy of production plans.

An average event has the highest probability , while the probability falls away on both sides as the individual events differ more and more from the average. The extent to which the curve spreads out is measured by a quantity called the 'standard deviation' (SD) of the distribution: 68 per cent of cases fall in the region between mean minus 1 sd and mean plus 1 SD while 96 per cent of cases fall in the region between mean minus 2 SD and mean plus 2 SD.

In the field of stock control, the mean can be taken as the average monthly usage of a stock item. As the curve falls away on the both sides, it can represent the probability that demand will differ from the average.

Records of stock usage can be used to find the mean and standard deviation of monthly usage for a particular item. Then, to guarantee a particular level of protection against stockout on that item it is necessary to have a safety stock of *K* times the standard deviation of monthly usage, where *K* is given by the table. It can be seen that achieving better protection against stockout requires an increasingly large investment in safety stocks.

Calculations of standard deviation demands access to detailed records must not only be accurate, but they must also relate to present-day production requirements. If the current situation is significantly changed from that which existed when the records were taken, any justification in figure computations.

K value	*Protection (%)*
0	50
0.84	80
1.04	85
1.28	90
1.41	92
1.56	94
1.75	96
2.05	98
2.33	99
2.57	99.5
2.88	99.8

Table of K values against stockout protection. Amount by which the standard deviation of monthly usage must be multiplied in order to achieve particular levels of protection against stockout

Converting production plans into stock requirements

Stock control embraces the provision of stores for all purposes from the single 'special' or project to materials used on continuous production. The basic necessity for any stock controller is the production plan for the year. This plan, derived from the marketing plan and agreeing with the annual budgets, must show the expected production rates for all products together with an estimation of the spare parts and replacement stocks to be carried.

Stock collation method for a single batch

For any particular stock item, the stock controller must know all the products or sub-assemblies on which it is used. This problem is simplest in the case of one special production batch or one product, where the provision of supplies only has to made for one production occasion. For any stock collation exercise the buyer or stock controller must start with a complete set of parts lists or bills of materials. The procedure in the case of a single project is simple, if tedious.

Consider a main assembly with the type number XYZ. The process of stock collation begins with he appropriate clerk checking through all the bills of materials. He must mark up the quantities on the main bill or materials to show the total number of items necessary to complete the entire batch. For example, if one main assembly needs twelve complete the entire batch. For example, if one main assembly needs twelve rivets type 1234, and 100 main assemblies are to be produced the clerk must rivets type 1234, and 100 main assemblies are to be produced the clerk must enter a net requirement of 1200 rivets on the bill of materials. This procedure must be repeated for every single item, whether it is manufactured or purchased, on the bill of materials.

The bill of materials for any sub-assembly listed on the main assembly must be treated in the same way. However, a further multiplication factor will be necessary if more than one sub-assembly is used on each main assembly. Suppose that two brackets type L Y are needed for each main assembly type X Y Z, then every single quantity listed on the bill of materials for the bracket must be multiplied by the total production quantity for the sub-assembly.

All of these quantities are written on to stock collation cards, one of which will be required for each item. When all the bills of materials have been processed, the quantities on all stock collation cards can be added up to find the net requirement for each item.

Stock collation system for a programme of mixed products

An extension of the system just described for single-batch working is seen in the production of a mixed product range. If common parts or sub-assemblies are shared between one or more of these mixed products and if production is continued on a repeating batch basis.

From the annual production plan the stock controller has to transfer the number of main assemblies to be produced into the column headings of a collation card. Individual sub-assemblies or parts required on each main assembly are then listed in the left-hand column, continuing on to further cards as necessary. From the relevant bills of materials, quantities of each part required on the main assembly are calculated and these are entered in the parts of the boxes above the diagonals. When this has been done it is then possible to consider each row on the form, and for every item to multiply the quantities shown as being required for each single main assembly by the annual usage figures. The results are entered in the parts of the boxes below the diagonals. After making an allowance for spares, accessories or wastage, the total annual usage for each item listed can be entered in the right-hand column.

This method is simple but somewhat crude. It does not attempt to phase requirements according to a timed programme but, if the company's policy is to hold at least three months' stock in advance, the method may be adequate. Should a more sophisticated system be required for relation total usage to a detailed daily or weekly production schedule the line-of-balance technique may be considered.

Stocktaking

Stocktaking is tedious/ and laborious chore that has to be performed annually to the satisfaction of the company's auditors in order to evaluate the quantities of stocks of materials and work in progress. The results are used in preparing the company's financial accounts and are also important for management control. Stocktaking verifies the accuracy of stock records and discloses possible frauds or other losses. The Inland Revenue and the auditors will need to be satisfied that suitable standards of accuracy are achieved. Some large organisation find it profitable to engage their own internal audit staff to undertake continuous stocktaking, but whether or not this is the case every company should practise stock checks periodically in between the major annual events.

Stocktaking needs careful planning to ensure that the whole exercise can be completed during the prescribed period. This is commonly arranged during a weekend or at some other time when production will not be interrupted. This is a necessary arrangement because stores receipts and issues have to be suspended while stocktaking is in progress. Because of the large amount of work involved all available staff have to be deployed. These will include people outside the normal stores function or people who have no connection with materials or even production during their normal working time. The role of storekeepers during stocktaking should be confined to that of guides so that the actual counting is always carried out by people who are independent of the usual stock records and stores functions. This is a safeguard against the perpetuation of errors or the concealment of possible fraud. The whole exercise can be supervised by the accounts.

Books of serially numbered tickets or, alternatively, pre-numbered list sheets have to provided. Serial numbering means that every ticket or sheet issued can be accounted for when the accountants come to top up all the values. The first step is for every item of stock, whether in the stores or on the factory floor, to be counted, either as a physical quantity or by weighing or measuring volume. The stores code or description is entered on a ticket together with the supervisory staff or other checkers make random checks of items already counted to verify the accuracy of the 'first-line' stocktaking staff. Finally the auditors themselves may wish to carry out their own counts on selected items. Naturally, more attention will be paid to the most expensive goods.

Stocktaking provides an opportunity. "which should not be missed, of identifying obsolete and redundant stocks the disposal of which can release both cash and space.

It is important to understand that the objective of stocktaking is not simply to verify the accuracy of stock records, but to assess the total value of stocks and work in progress. This means that all stocks have to be counted and valued, including materials, components and assemblies throughout the factory and its stores and stockyards. The value of these items is not represented solely by the material stocks contained in them; the investment of wages and salaries used in all work in progress has to be included.

10 Purchasing and Suppliers

The relationship between a library or information unit and a supplier can cover a whole range of associations from a single order that goes disastrously wrong to a long and mutually rewarding association in which the library is provided with material reliably and on time, and the supplier receives a just financial payback. It is the librarian's role to ensure that the organization being served achieves the best possible outcome from the association, although the problem is, of course, that the 'best' is defined by a cumulation of requirements that each supplier must meet in order to have a satisfied client. An unsatisfied client not only produces irritations and eventually a loss of business, but the poor reputation of the supplier may spread of other potential clients.

Some of the criticism may be unjustified, resulting from unreasonable expectations by the library. It is therefore in the interests of the supplier as much as the supplied that the two parties agree on the materials to be supplied, services on offer, and conditions of delivery. While contract law has developed to define many of these relationships, it often manages to achieve the dual sins of being both too detailed and too crude in its methods. For instance, in an obscure on-line service you use twice a year there may be three pages of microscopic detail in a contract, whereas the definitions of service provision between you and your main supplier of books and journals may be very brief and lacking in detail. Can you find your contract now? If you can find it, you keep it with you at all times. But is it still relevant?

Cost differentials are often limited in book and journal supply, and the service elements of the relationship governed by unwritten and changing circumstances. The apparent efficiency of the library can be greatly influenced by the ability of the supplier to produce the items required on time. This chapter considers some of the most important elements in the selection of suppliers, the relevance of the continuing relationship, and the mutual support that produces good quality results. We look at what it is worth in terms of saving the time of the library, saving money, and delivering faster than the next supplier. The problem for the supplier is, of course, that they can provide any level of service that the client requires, but at a cost either in terms of money or as a depletion of facilities. In many ways it is the client's responsibility to make clear exactly what is required in a structured way so that the potential supplier can produce a package that states costs and service, and which can be measured and monitored effectively.

The process of selection implies some form of competition, either directly in terms of a tendering process, or in terms of measuring the comparative performance of different sources. The client therefore needs to be able to determine the value and types of service, how this is to be measured and over what period, and the way in which samples, analyses and the results of analyses are to be determined. Added to this will be the opinions of other users of the supplier, and the ways in which they match or do not match needs.

Our 'supplier' may be one of any number of sources for the materials and services we require. Of course, there is a continued debate in the mind of anyone charged with purchasing—go to source or use an agent. In the end the decision is usually taken out of our control, for which many of us are grateful. Certain sources of supply decide that they trade only directly with the final receiver of the material, a not uncommon attitude among those who produce market analyses, while others insist that an appointed agent must be the access route within a particular geographical area. Between these two extremes the purchaser can, however, exercise considerable judgement on the sources for information and the techniques and methods those suppliers use.

The initial reaction of those who see library systems for the first time is often 'Why use an agent? It's quicker to go direct." It is only after some thought that the overheads involved in a total 'source from originator' policy appear to be less attractive. We perhaps dismiss this naive approach too easily, since it often emanates from senior members of the organization who may go away unconvinced by a dismissive librarian. Time spent discussing the priorities for employee time not only answers specific queries, but transmits to the receiver that the librarian understands the need to manage their operations effectively.

Single or multiple suppliers?

The decision on the number of suppliers to use, one or many, is often taken from the library, since there are inevitably suppliers who will not deal with an agent and insist that orders come from source. For the majority of orders which pass through the system, however, the client, i.e. the library, does have the choice as to whether only one main supplier is employed, or two or more. The ability to match two suppliers against each other is at first attractive, but will the comparison be fair, since it can be difficult to directly measure success unless they all receive an even distribution of orders in terms of quantity and difficulty? The multiple supplier situation can be difficult to evaluate, but the monopoly supplier is even more of a problem as no comparison can be made except by inference from colleagues whose data will be difficult to interpret. The rationale for the monopoly situation is the greater influence that the client has, but that in turn leaves the library dependent on one source. Any efforts to improve the service of such a supplier are fraught with difficulties, since a basis for comparison does not exist.

The suppliers we deal with here fall into three broad areas:

- suppliers of single order items such as books, reports and similar documents, equipment, etc.
- suppliers of repeat business such as journals and standing orders
- suppliers of services.

Criteria for choosing suppliers

Accounting and financial concerns

In many ways, the library being served by a trader is not in a simple client-seller relationship. The library serves a company or other organization which is supported by its orders and accounts department. While these are themselves designed to provide a service to other parts of the organization, their relationship with the rest is deeply affected by the reliance which is placed on accounts to ensure that the flow of resources in and out of the organization is regulated to provide for the continuation and development of the company. What others may see as a simple clerical procedure masks the complexities of company law and cash flow. Anything another section can do to minimize perturbations in the systems that govern the financial dealings of the organization will earn appreciation from these custodians of the purse, and be repaid many times.

First, of course, one needs to gain the confidence of the accountants, establishing a relationship in which mutual skills are respected and built up to provide for the smooth running of company systems and the reduction of individual work problems.

On normal order and payment routines, techniques and systems need to be established with primary suppliers that match the requirements of the company's accountants. Every slide in the system produced by a non-standard accountancy procedure results in a disproportional amount of effort for all. Suppliers need to understand the company's accountancy needs in detail, and the consequences to the organization of not meeting them. Such three-way co-operation enables company employees to focus on those areas where compliance with the organization's needs are not so easily established. There will be suppliers with whom it is difficult to build up such a relationship, including the large on-line hosts, government publishers, and organizations which demand direct orders and will not go through agents. With these sources, which often operate within their own intricate and usually mystifying methods, the 'mutual aid method' built up with the internal accounting section when dealing with regular suppliers will smooth the handling of these difficult to administer accounts.

Other aspects of the payments systems that are of concern include the amount of time from invoicing to payment expected by the supplier, any penalties for late payment, and any incentives for early payment. While many companies operate on the basis of paying only at the last moment, in the supply areas in which we exist the cash flow of the supplier may materially affect delivery performance.

Foreign currency transactions are a major problem for companies unused to operating in the international arena, and providing invoices in the local currency for materials from many sources is one of the most 'value added' services a supplier can render. Converting currencies, obtaining orders, and clearing cash through foreign banks not only save time and effort, but reduce risks for the purchaser. The costs of such activities must, however, be borne by someone, and the purchase price may be heavily loaded to recover the time that has been expended. From time to time correspondence appears in the library press which indicates differences in prices for the same item by as much as 100% for the end purchaser. On sets of expensive specialist encyclopaedia and continuing series this difference can amount to a significant sum.

Understanding the basis on which suppliers charge for foreign material can therefore save thousands over the course of a year. Suppliers with established links in the countries in which the material you are seeking is published stand the best chance of obtaining such material at a good price, and also in reasonable time. How and whether they pass on the financial benefits or costs is a matter of negotiation between them and you. You should at least know on what basis currency conversion rates are calculated, and how any supplement for foreign material is introduced.

Without this you cannot even begin to assess the costs and benefits of the service you are seeking.

Bibliographically speaking

The timely and accurate provision of material relies to a large extent on the accuracy and completeness of the information generated by the originator of an order and the ability of the supplier to reinforce and supplement this information. Many suppliers see the provision of an accurate and complete bibliographic service as a major feature in their strategy. Evaluating the strength and utility of such services is one of the most difficult aspects of customer/supplier relationships. In many cases the customer may be supporting a service which is not really required. Often the information given on a customer's original order is sufficient and accurate enough to enable the item to be supplied immediately. On others the very nature of the material and lack of information may defeat the intermediate supplier just as much as the originator.

On the other hand, the supplier that can rapidly locate and supply an obscure, urgently required item scores well. Only experience can provide a guide to the benefits using any one supplier can bring to such a situation, although information on the skills and sources available to them will give a strong clue. There is, however, little benefit from receiving a service you do not need, and if you have confidence in your own bibliographic resources you should find a supplier who will offer alternative plus points. A mutual understanding of the bibliographic tools regularly employed by both parties and a common set of codes to denote sources checked will at least prevent needless duplication of effort and eliminate time wasted in repeated checking.

But I want it now

A supplier must decide to what extent the client is driven by price, and to what extent by the level of service on offer. The problem is, of course, that the needs of each client are different, and the needs of those individual clients vary depending on their end users. This is an almost impossible problem for the supplier to solve without adequate information from the client, since without this information the supplier is being asked to make a value judgement about an unknown end use. Tactics employed include librarians trusting that supplier goodwill be generated by placing regular orders and suppliers making a feature of rapid service at a premium price, e.g. same day delivery of new HMSO materials.

An alternative to either of these tactics is to establish an understanding between the normal supplier and the client on a *modus operandi* for urgent orders. Many delays can be minimized if a basic set of rules is negotiated between both parties on the procedures each will follow if an item is designated urgent. If the proportion of urgent to non-urgent orders is also broadly agreed as a percentage of overall trading, rapid delivery may be achieved when needed at a negligible premium price. The occasion when your Managing Director calls for an obscure document required yesterday is not the time to start talks with your suppliers.

In addition to determining price and delivery such negotiations may cover:

- who is the client's organizations can declare an item urgent
- the level of information supplied about the item.
- any special protocols for delivery. For example, should all urgent orders be faxed through to the supplier to avoid any misunderstandings a telephone call might introduce?

Even with the urgent action specialist suppliers, clearance of credit and an understanding of their trading techniques can be as effective as any other element in ensuring prompt service.

But its not here...

While the aim of all suppliers is to deliver items required at an appropriate time, the efficient notification of possible delays has great value. Not only does it reduce the frustration of the client, but it enables them to plan for the delay. Reports on the factors involved in a delay need to be in a form which is easily assimilated into the client's own record system, and in a form that can be transmitted on to their users with the minimum of effort. The client and the supplier need to establish the events and timescales that lead to the production of reports, and the regularity with which they are produced should an item have a long delay. There should be arrangements made to cover situations where prices are above those predicted by the library.

Stock exchange

Most of the time the fact that a supplier holds stock may not be relevant, since the normal distribution system will enable the supplier to order directly from source and to deliver in what the client perceives is a satisfactory timescale. The stockholder has additional overheads in terms of the stock itself and the storage needed to hold it in readiness for orders. By definition, they will have material on the shelves that is going to be in demand and is therefore in the category of 'less difficult to obtain' material. The non-stockholder can concentrate staff on ordering material rather than supporting that which is in stock, and as a result may have a quicker turnaround on the majority of orders not recovered from stock and at a lower cost. The selection of a specialist stockholder thus becomes one of the more finely balanced decision making activities, since their value lies in their ability to 'second-guess' your needs—which they are unlikely to know unless you have been a customer over a considerable period. A sample from some recent orders to your existing supplier can provide an indication of the potential a supplier has in your field for immediate delivery. However, remember that urgently required material may not be mainstream in your subject area, but may be specialist material such as government documents or standards.

An efficient selective dissemination of information (SDI) service on new publications within the library's interest domain provides the supplier's client with an economical method of checking that the library is keeping up with new material. If this information is supplied in a form that matches the library's administrative systems, perhaps as paper slips or a machine readable file, the service can become an integral element in the library's information provision activities.

A good supplier should be able to provide assistance during stock building and editing by the production of lists of suitable material both in stock and not in stock but in print. An inspection service provides this type of support on a continuing basis, although care is needed in establishing the exact conditions under which the service is provided.

The benefits of a book servicing facility will be dependent on the amount of material acquired in a year. For some the amount of inhouse time saved by a supplier placing stationary and stamps in new material will be insignificant, while for others the savings enable other tasks to be accomplished in-house that could otherwise not be carried out. Similarly, differences in the charges made for these activities may be a significant element in selecting a supplier. Delivery costs, packaging, etc., all add to costs. In the end it is the price at the bottom of the invoice that we need to concentrate on.

Delivery is a matter not only of efficient

service to your clients, but has a direct effect on the allocation of staff resources. A delivery cycle which is unreliable, sporadic and infrequent leaves the purchaser with the inability to plan work loads and causes delays right up to the final payment of invoices. Even if we cannot control individual one-off suppliers, we should be able to obtain a reasonable delivery arrangement from regular ones.

Contract renewal

Few events fill the manager with more dread than going out to contract for the supply of periodicals and standing orders through an agent. Among the most prominent of the more hated experiences is managing the process which stems from using a new agent, i.e. the transition period from the old supplier. While some organizations leave the style and timing for going through the tendering process to the information officer or librarian, in other this event appears to be just the opportunity for the company purchasing officers to show off their skills. If the organization's style is to utilize the talents of purchase/order departments fully in the process, then the secret is, of course, to involve them on your terms. Indeed, such sections have skills that are important and useful, they just perhaps need some moderating.

Seize the initiative by approaching the relevant person early on in the process, and making it clear you value and respect their professional help. A clear understanding of aspects of a tender not directly concerned with price is important. By making a list of these points and placing an estimate of value on them you will be able to more easily isolate the differences between one quotation and another. Having established a document based not only on price but on system responses, such as dealing with missing issues. invoices, credit arrangements, etc., suppliers can be asked to present their offerings. An establlished track record with similar clients is an important element. Some quantification of the cost of switching from the existing source should be made, and of the help a prospective supplier could give in effecting the transfer. This is a good point at which to discuss the results of any possible change of supplier with the current agent. While the tendering process is being conducted, the existing supplier is much more likely to agree the possible ending of a relationship on amicable terms.

When tenders are examined they can be evaluated against your criteria and the successful agent established. One of the options in this process will of course be a fully estimated and costed alternative to conducting the purchase of periodicals and standing orders directly from source. Once the decision on a supplier has been made, 'those who failed to get the contract should be informed of the reasons for their failure, provided company policy permits this. Such feedback gives those unsuccessful suppliers an opportunity to improve their techniques and increase the chances of success next time. One of the advantages of having an established cycle of going out to tender and communicating this to suppliers is that those who lose out on the current evaluation know the framework in which another opportunity will arise.

Measuring the differences

Determining the 'best' supplier for a service depends on the ability to measure the performance of the organization itself against a set of criteria. The assessment of the supplier's performance against those criteria which are the most sensitive produces a set of performance indicators. Performance indicators have been widely advocated by those who control library budgets in all sectors, so developing them for libraries to use in comparing their performance to other libraries gives a new insight into their relevance, as well as helping to define a set of measurable objectives for suppliers to fulfill.

Our supplier performance indicators can be developed from the criteria already discussed. They will enable the library both to compare the supplier against targets assigned to individual companies, and to compare one company with another.

Even with a small throughput of new material the ability to answer the question 'How well does my supplier do?' except in the most general terms, requires the processing power that a computer can give. This sounds relatively easy: but a package-there are enough acquisition and order modules available for even small operations to implement. Unfortunately, most of these see the type of management information we need as secondary to the task of processing transactions, such as posting an order or invoice to the system. The position is beginning to change, but the requirement for complex analysis of time is still a challenge that many systems are unable to meet.

Even if such analysis is possible, be careful that differences in suppliers are not masking differences in environments and demands. The amount of effort required for such a sophisticated approach needs to be matched by benefits which may not be in the delivery of all materials x days early, but in the arrival of just one important item on time as a result of knowing who best to choose for the order.

Automating your suppliers

It is, of course, one of the tenets of modern library automation that automating the links between supplier and library will lead to improved cost efficiency and service effectiveness. This is simpler to say than to achieve given that there are currently few operational standards to which suppliers can provide a common interface. Some are in the process of development, but until these have reached full international standards status, linking your automated system to that of your supplier is a matter of negotiation. Where you use several suppliers, each of which has a number of other clients, a standard method of communication may seem impossible. A simple file transfer format such as a series of fields in sequential order in ASCII file format may, however, produce an interim measure that provides a pay off in terms of staff time saved at both the library and the supplier, and which more than recoups the effort expended in developing such a system. Not only does such downloading of files in the form of discs or through electronic mail speed up clerical processes, but it leads to greater accuracy by eliminating keyboarding and rechecking data.

Remote hosts

The term remote database was coined to define the geographic relationship between the information store and the end user. It is often also an accurate description of the type of relationship enjoyed by the user. Such hosts have very carefully defined terms and conditions of service, originally developed with little thought to the user, which can be imposed quite easily by threat of removing the service instantly using the database password administration system. 'Invalid password' or 'access denied' can be the first indication one has that the organization's accounts system has failed to make a payment on time.

Some of these database hosts were originally targeted on individuals rather than companies, or were set up for the US market where the use of credit cards for business accounts is much more widespread. The payment method is therefore geared to this, and other methods of handling accounts are treated as secondary. Attempting to persuade your organization to have a charge account or credit card for such payments is probably a challenge which you see as having limited prospects of success, but it is worth thoroughly enumerating the benefits of such a tactic as the advantages to your organization could easily outweigh any company general policy about payments made this way. There is little you can do to establish an easy relationship with these remote on-line suppliers, but some planning may help.

Individual problems can be more easily dealt with if a local agent or office is in place. Failing this, try to establish the name and location of a person who will deal with any problems you have at the host. A fax number will yield great benefits in establishing rapid communications, as will the electronic mailbox of the link person if the on-line host includes e-mail in its facilities.

Changing a supplier's administrative and accounting procedures which are wasteful and inconvenient for the end user by taking up the matter as an individual client is perhaps the method least likely to work. Rather more profitable is to join a user group: both groups designed around particular hosts and more general on-line user groups enable pressure to be applied and problems to be dealt with in a concerted and organized way. Suppliers are then much more likely to act.

Purchasing automated systems

Until a comparatively few years ago the largest contract and purchase that a library needed to be involved in was the periodic review of journal subscriptions. Now, the purchase of automated systems and their attendant maintenance equal and surpass this. The problem is, of course, that while journals are an area every librarian has confidence in, the supply of automated systems produces less confidence and may be heavily biased by company policy on information technology. In addition to the involvement of orders and accounts staff, computing staff may also become involved.

Not that the basic principles of purchase change, but new factors are introduced. A specification of requirements is still needed, and tenders invited and measured on the basis of costs and services, in this case facilities and performance. Questions of deliverables and support are, however, even more important than in normal purchase arrangements. There is also the need to define the requirements for systems now and also over the next five to ten years. There is not usually the luxury of being able to carry out an annual review in this area, and cut or increase facilities to match the budget. Money will still have to be found to support the system in five years' time no matter what level the disposable budget. It is at this point that we need to discuss the full cost of system support over the period of its planned use—its life-cycle cost, including input from your own personnel. While suppliers are often cautious about projecting forward such figures, they become less sensitive to the matter if they understand that every potential supplier has to produce some justified data.

Two of the main reasons that computer system installation plans go wrong are over-specification and 'vapourware'. These exemplify a simple but often repeated problem of not building a relationship with potential suppliers. Both result from the failure to achieve an understanding of the balance between facilities, investment and growth. By over-specifying a system in a tender document, the library may eliminate perfectly suitable and often superior systems from competing. At first sight it may seem a good tactic to specify every possible facility you may wish to use eventually, and require it to be immediately available. In this way, each potentially useful element in the system can be seen to work before purchase. Without such an approach you could be buying 'vapourware', i.e. a part of the system which, although planned, does not exist as a product.

Both approaches lead to failure. The first assumes that your unit will take up all the elements in the system almost immediately, probably something which it is organizationally unable to do. In the period between contract signing and uptake of service, some products may have moved on in specification and so no longer match your needs. One of the rival systems originally rejected may now appear to be more suitable. On the other hand, buying on a company's promises of future products can lead to disappointment if the plans are not fulfilled on schedule.

The careful potential system purchaser discusses the department's mid-term plans and resources, levels to build a picture of implementation for the system. In this way, both parties can establish event points along a pathway to full system adoption and mark those points in such a way that each understands the other's role and obligations. Such a policy will also enable each party to assess the needs for hardware growth and upgrade during the life of the system.

Computer systems require a high level of support, both hardware and software, over their life time. The potential purchaser needs to know just how that support is to be offered, and the terms under which it is offered. Some protection needs to be given to the client if the company should fail, such as access to the computer code used and the availability of alternative maintenance sources.

Using information brokers

The information broker's role in an organization's information unit can be ambivalent. On the one hand they may be seen as an aid, while on the other they may appear to be potential alternative sources of information for the parent organization.

The broker has a definite role within an established information unit, able to provide a service within three broad areas: the provision of specialist skills which it is not economic for the unit to support, access to sources that the company may not have directly, and the delivery of information under time constraints that the information unit may be unable to meet because of a sudden temporary upturn in demand.

The cost to an information unit of supporting certain skills with training and practice can be high if the source concerned is little used. Taking all these staff and support costs into consideration, a broker's 'value added' fee may be economical. Brokers acting as third parties can trace information where a direct approach may be rejected.

Although brokers will of course act on a one-off call basis to a standard set of conditions and a fee, building up a relationship with a broker will enable you to assess their talents and be better able to decide when they should be called in. You need to know how each broker handles an enquiry. Do they specialize in certain areas—most do—and what action is taken if an enquiry does not match their skills profile? Some will direct clients to other sources; if so, who do they recommend and why? Do they have reciprocal arrangements with these other sources?

Alternatively, do they sub-contract work to others under their own trading name? If so, to whom, and is the client told when this is done and to whom the work is sent? If the broker uses people who do not work exclusively for them, then who else do they work for, and to whom are they connected? While brokers will not knowingly break a confidence, a chain of people that extends to the interests of a rival company is to be avoided. A chain of subcontractors will also add to cost overheads and make dealing with any subsequent matters that may arise out of the initial enquiry difficult.

Who needs a consultant?

The role of consultants is often maligned by those who have experienced the arrival, and subsequent departure, of a person who seems full of instant answers but has no responsibility for any outcomes of recommendations. Such experiences are usually the fault of the organizations bringing in the consultant rather than the consultants themselves.

A consultant may be brought in for particular skills, to bring a new approach to a problem, perhaps by looking at a reorganization; or may be asked to give a second opinion on a situation or suggestion. To develop good relations with a consultant one needs to understand the nature of the consultancy, be able to communicate this effectively, and be able to structure the outcome so that any recommendations can be effectively examined by the organization's management, commented on, and appropriate action taken.

The whole process is more likely to develop smoothly if it is the information manager rather than anyone else in the organization who decides that a consultant should be employed within the unit. If this is followed up with a short-list of possible individuals who could fulfil the role, then the initiative, once established, can be built on.

A document setting out the contractual terms of the consultancy and a definition of the area to be covered will enable the short-list of possible consultants to respond with a quotation on the size and cost of the work. When the consultant has been selected they will need more detailed background on the existing situation, the organization, and the roles and relationships between people within it. The success of a consultancy stems to a large extent from building mutual confidence between the consultant and those within the organization with whom they come into contact.

The consultant will understand this, and work towards it as a major goal in achieving the stated aims of the mission. It is those who have never experienced such a situation, or those who have been involved in a poor consultancy, who need support, and it is the section leader who can best provide this through a knowledge of the motivations of those who will be most affected by any outcome. The consultant is only too aware of being both a temporary employee and someone who may change the local environment drastically, both at the same time.

11 Records Keeping

Records management may be defined as the systematic control of records from the point of their creation to the point either of their destruction or inclusion in an archive. But what actually is a record? According to Alexis de Toqueville, writing early last century on public administration in the United States, records were paper documents. For Schellenberg in the 1950s, records comprised much the same material, although his definition was more elaborate: records were:

> 'correspondence, memoranda... statistical tabulations and analyses, performance and accomplishment reports, narrative reports, and the like that contain the information needed for making decisions; circulars, memoranda, and other procedural and policy directives that serve as means of administrative control; selected records of past actions that serve as precedents...'

What constitutes a record?

By the 1980s, however, the definition of what

constituted a record had changed beyond all measure. According to one modern authority, records comprised,'any paper, book, photograph, microfilm, map, drawing, chart, magnetic tape or disk, or optical disk. Even this definition appeared dated by 1991, since it failed to specify either electronic mail or databases.

As these illustrations suggest, perceptions of what a record actually is have changed radically and rapidly. In the past, records were just papers, and records management might be perceived as a part of archival administration. Nowadays, the record is as likely to be an electronic impulse as a piece of paper, and the records manager is often recruited from the ranks of information scientists or computer systems architects.

Nevertheless, these important changes should not obseure the fact that one of the principal problems facing records managers is much the same as in de Toqueville's day: paper documents in such volume as to be virtually unmanageable. The electronic office has not led to the creation of the paperless office. In fact, since executives have a tendency to constantly redraft on line and to print off each version for distribution, the electronic office has led to a proliferation of paperwork. Also, of course, it is far easier to compose on-line than to write on paper. The development of modern computerized systems has thus paradoxically created new difficulties in the handling of the most traditional medium of communication.

The impact of legislation

Additionally, we need to consider the impact of legislation. Year by year, UK and European Community statutes apply to the type of material which has to be retained for legal reasons. Apart from the Companies' Acts, Local Government Acts and Finance Acts, which are enough in themselves, there are at least 20 other statutory instruments covering the retention of organizational records. As companies expand their operations they have to consider the impact of foreign legislation on the type of records they keep. In addition, with the advent of the single European market, companies will need to be able to prove that they have not been infringing European competition law or been engaged in transborder price-fixing. Officials of the EC Commission or of the UK's Department of Trade and Industry have the right to enter premises unannounced and to examine books or other business records. If there are gaps in the accounts then the company is liable for heavy fines and the company secretary risks imprisonment. To offset this dire eventuality, companies are bound to retain much more than is really needed.

Records systems and the organization's needs

The basic aim of records management is as follows: to ensure that the information necessary for running a business can be retrieved efficiently. Most organizations do not bother to think of records management until they either lose a vital contract or cannot find the papers they need in a convenient space of time. Once this happens they define the conditions as urgent, recruit or appoint a records manager, and implement a records management programme. The outcome will usually be a disaster: the newly appointed manager will either impose a copy-cat system learned elsewhere, or will read too many textbooks and attend too many expensive conferences urging the introduction of a comprehensive, 'Rolls-Royce' solution. In fact, the 'old banger' which works is just as good.

Most organizations simply need to identify their immediate priorities and develop a system to meet their needs. A minicab office does not need an elaborate system for invoice-control, nor does it require a safe-storage programme for vital records. Many organizations do not need on-line connection to commercial databases, or a highly centralized filing system. Experience shows that most organizations, once they have identified the problem of the paper mountain and published guidelines to good practice, have resolved most of their difficulties. The records manager will therefore spend most of his/her time hunting our opportunities for storage, drawn up forms to facilitate retrieval, advising on how long documents need to be kept for legal and financial reasons, and organizing the disposal of confidential waste. Few should be involved in composing a company-wide filing system, or in hauling filing cabinets into a new central registry.

Contrary to the popular perception,. most records can be safely left with the departments that either generate or use them. All that the records manager needs to do is to advise on good practice and provide support with regard to storage and security. Vital records, however, need to be identified and retained under conditions of safety. Often all this requires is a safe and a security classification scheme which is not abused by prestige-seekers. It does not require a vault on the other side of the world.

In addition, if departments are made responsible in the first instance for their records, they can then be billed for storage costs incurred. This has the advantage of obliging departments to determine for themselves what ought to be kept. If the records manager assumes the burden of having to work out that ought to be kept for five, ten or twenty years, he or she will soon be involved in endless wrangles over whether or not the 1982 Christmas party expenses account needs to be retained. This account has, after all, a deeply historical and sentimental value, and may also be useful in plotting long-term trends in consumption. Should it not be kept for just a little longer?

Automation

Some of the most useful advice the records manager can give lies in regard to computerized information systems. There is, of course, a problem with any sort of computerization. Most people think they are experts on the performance of the English football team, and most believe the same with regard to the latest techniques in automation. Men are particularly bad in this respect, since the use of computing terminology is considered *de regueur* for the thrusting male executive. The records manager will need to be particularly knowledgeable and convincing if he or, especially, she is to cut through the layers of self-defeating presumption.

The first and most obvious benefit of computerization lies in regard to the retention of outgoing correspondence. Letters and minutes drafted on-line can be safely stored in the creating word processor. If the computers in an organization are networked, then internal communications need never be printed on to hard copy, and there can be common access to files through a file server. Since, however, viruses abound and accidents are commonplace, the printing out of important correspondence should be made mandatory.

As yet, however, there are few facilities for transferring incoming paper correspondence into electronic form. Scanning is slow, expensive and not always satisfactory. A recent development is the digitizing camera which transfers an image on to diskette. This technology is still in its infancy, but in five years' time it will doubtless be commonplace not only in the office but in the home.

In five years' time, however, most organizations will have dispensed with the Post Office and fax and will be communicating one to another through electronic mailing systems and optical fibre cables. Already, for example, universities in the UK are doing this through the JANET network. Once this happens, informing as well as outgoing communications may all be stored on-line. The records manager of the future will need to be able to advise on consistency of electronic filing and subject-tagging. He or she will also need to consider whether seldom used information is stored in a format where it can be summoned electronically or as a disk/CD-ROM which is kept in a central area and retrieved manually.

Where an organization relies upon a large number of files of standard type, it is possible to retain these on microfiche or on optical disk. As far as the former is concerned, the lead in this technology was taken at an early stage by insurance companies, library cataloguers and technical suppliers. The advantage of both technologies is that they reduce volume very substantially, and are easily filed and retrieved, often in conjunction with a colour coding or header system. Both media may also be prepared on-line, and the relevant image may be summoned up electronically. The legal validity of the records so stored, however, gives pause for thought.

The latest technology allows all these various options to be used simultaneously on the screen. With a 'Windows' facility, the operator may summon up information held on disk, on CD-ROM and on microfiche all at the same time. He or she will not have to long-off before moving on to the next option. Crucially, however, the new technology also allows the operator to gain access to outside databases. It is in this respect that the traditional perception of records management is changing the most rapidly.

Integration with information management

In the past, the records manager dealt primarily with internally generated records that were more than often past their very active life. Now, however, as the executive charged with providing 'the information necessary to run a business', the records manager is becoming increasingly involved with providing access not only to the store of informatiaon generated within the organization, but also to a variety of outside databases. Databases available include most obviously news services, press digests, and market reports. This commercial information can be integrated into the work being carried out on-line by the operator, and into the internal records of the organization. Thus, for instance, the daily price of widgets can be included and modified on a spreadsheet, which is then incorporated into the company's own sales records. The records manager thus becomes an information manager, distributing and manipulating information of varied provenance.

Nevertheless, this additional responsibility imposes new burdens on the records manager. Not only will he or she have to be abreast of the latest technology and commercial initiatives, but the manager will also have to assume responsibility for managing contracts with the commercial database hosts, for monitoring costs, and for ensuring that copyright is not breached. The last of these is a potential minefield. To give one example: if the organization contracts to receive a daily review of the international widget market from Textline and this review is distributed to ten widget traders, legally the organization has bought from Textline not one but eleven copies.

As the records/information manager becomes over more closely involved with the provision of current information, so his or her role becomes more akin to that of the information scientist/ librarian. By the same token, the old link with the archivist becomes increasingly tenuous. The archivist was historically concerned with the management of dead records, the records manager with semi-active ones, which were usually internally generated. Now, however, in the wider role of information manager, the records manager is providing current information from internal and external sources.

When is a document a document?

The overlap between records management and information management carries with it a profound philosophical problem: When is a document a document? As data progresses from network to network, and the text expands, contracts and alters, at what point is the document actually formed? Until now we have always known what a document was. It had a clearly visible format, and we could hold it in our hands. These qualities are, however, lost once the document is on-line. Once a message ceases to be printed in paper form and simply flashes on a screen, it loses some of the qualities which in the past made it easily identifiable as something which ought to be retained and 'managed. As technical drawings are updated on the computer-design system, as commercial data is buzzed around the management-information system, and is integrated with internal sources, when is the stage reached for, as it were, a 'photograph' to be taken of that information for retention?

In the past transmission of thought to paper was the crucial stage in document production. Now, however, thoughts are transmitted to disk, revised both by the creator and by other staff members, and combined with new information. The text may be constantly 'saved' and 'sent' but it may never be printed out or logged on the company filing system. We are thus moving into a twilight world where the entire documentation process becomes an extension of the human brain. As I have noted elsewhere.

> 'On-line documents are the ghosts of a reasoning process still unconsummated. The circuit is the neuron writ large; and the "document" may now be no more distinguished than a thought.'

At what point should these thoughts be isolated from the mental processes which give them their being, and be scheduled for retention? Almost certainly, as the concept of the 'document' becomes extended, we will have to find an alternative definition of what constitutes a document. At some point procedures will have to be laid down or inculcated, so that the creator recognizes the existing text to have acquired a sufficient significance for the process of revision to be suspended and for the text to be frozen in its current form ready for retention. If this is not done, it is entirely possible to imagine a situation when all that emerges as retained text from a project is the final report. The working papers and data, background briefs, terms of reference, policy initiatives and management interventions have all been cut and pasted into the final text, and have lost their discrete identity as individual information items. A conventional audit trail under these circumstances becomes almost impossible.

If the creator cannot or will not do this, or there are so many creators at work that consensus in impossible, the records manager will have to intervene and arrange for the freezing of texts. *Entia no sint multiplicanda sine necessitate*: but, with due respect to Ockham, the necessity is upon us. In law, the distinction between 'corporate records' and the processes which gave these records birth is already blurred. In the United States, the category of *corporate record* is now extended to include all on-line data: messages, notes, and textualized ideas. To what extent do these new categories actually have a real existence? Will the problems attending their reification be considered at all valid in a court of law?

Records management stands today at a critical moment. The idea that records are just paper is no longer true, even though the electronic revolution has paradoxically created not less but more paperwork. The records manager is involved at the hard end of computer technology, and should be familiar with the latest developments and aware of their impact upon the discipline of management. He/she is now as much an intermediary for current information as a person who looks after semi-active documents. Beyond all this, however, the records manager will need to assume a much more active role in getting departments to release information. He/she will have to intervene constantly in the creative process to extract information for retention.

Index